BEYOND COLD SHOWERS

A COMPREHENSIVE GUIDE TO THE WIM HOF METHOD AND ITS BENEFITS

HUNTER HAZELTON

LIFE LEVEL UP BOOKS, LLC

Beyond Cold Showers: A Comprehensive Guide to the Wim Hof Method and Its Benefits

Copyright © 2023 by Hunter Hazelton

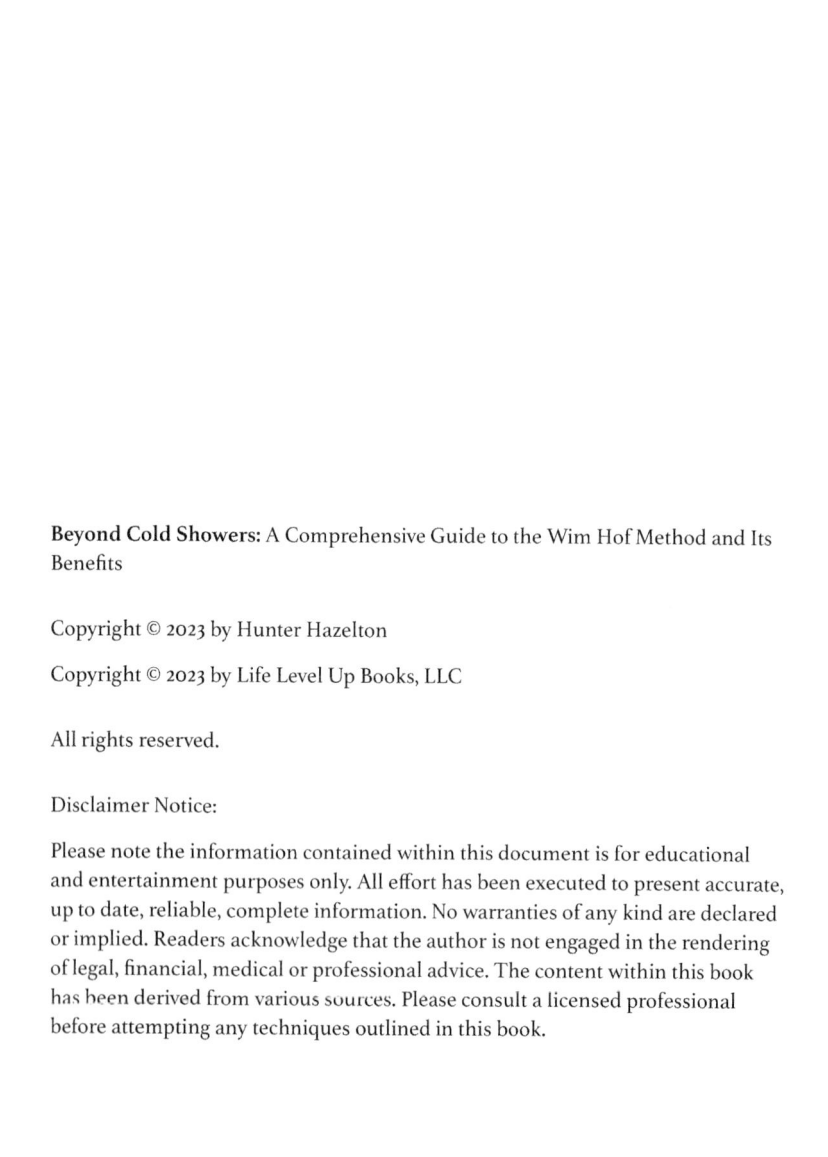

Copyright © 2023 by Life Level Up Books, LLC

All rights reserved.

Disclaimer Notice:

Please note the information contained within this document is for educational and entertainment purposes only. All effort has been executed to present accurate, up to date, reliable, complete information. No warranties of any kind are declared or implied. Readers acknowledge that the author is not engaged in the rendering of legal, financial, medical or professional advice. The content within this book has been derived from various sources. Please consult a licensed professional before attempting any techniques outlined in this book.

CONTENTS

Introduction	1
1. Discovering the Wim Hof Method	5
A Path to Extraordinary Health	
2. Breathing to Energize	14
Mastering the Wim Hof Breathing Technique	
3. Cold Exposure	24
Unleashing Your Inner Warrior	
4. Mindfulness and Meditation	34
Enhancing Focus and Clarity	
5. Uniting the Pillars	44
Combining Breathing, Cold, and Mindfulness	
6. Nutrition for Optimal Performance	53
Fueling Your Wim Hof Journey	
7. Boosting Athletic Performance	63
Elevating Your Fitness with the Wim Hof Method	
8. Cultivating Resilience	73
Overcoming Stress and Anxiety with the Wim Hof Method	
9. The Wim Hof Method for All Ages	83
Adapting the Practice for Different Life Stages	
10. The Wim Hof Lifestyle	93
Embracing a Holistic Approach to Health and Well-Being	
Conclusion	103

SOLARTURNSMEON.COM

SKY HIGH ENERGY BILL?

Stop Renting Your Energy, Own It Just Like You Own Your Home

- Solar for **$0 down**
- **Save up to $200/mo** on energy
- **Increase** your home value
- Get **clean renewable energy**
- Get a **30-year warranty**
- **Customized** proposal & best value

INTRODUCTION

Imagine a life brimming with vitality, purpose, and joy—a life in which you harness the power of your breath, embrace the invigorating cold, and cultivate a mindset that allows you to triumph over adversity. This is the life that awaits those who embark on the transformative journey of the Wim Hof Method. Through a unique combination of breathwork, cold exposure, and mindset training, this method holds the key to unlocking your fullest potential and living a life of purpose and fulfillment.

THE WIM HOF METHOD is a groundbreaking approach to holistic wellness that has captured the attention and imagination of people worldwide. Developed by Dutch extreme athlete Wim Hof, nicknamed the "Iceman" for his incredible feats in extreme cold environments, the method has been scientifically proven to bolster the immune system, reduce inflammation, and enhance mental clarity. The benefits, however, extend far beyond the physical realm, as the method's principles can profoundly impact our emotional well-being and overall sense of purpose.

AT THE HEART of the Wim Hof Method lies the power of breathwork. Our breath is an often overlooked, yet essential component of our well-being. By learning to control and optimize our breathing, we can tap into a wellspring of energy, relaxation, and mental clarity. The Wim Hof Method's unique breathing exercises enable us to access deeper states of consciousness, strengthen our immune response, and manage stress effectively. By exploring and mastering the power of our breath, we open the door to a more balanced, purposeful, and fulfilling life.

COLD EXPOSURE IS another fundamental aspect of the Wim Hof Method. By willingly subjecting ourselves to cold temperatures, we not only trigger a cascade of physiological adaptations that boost our overall health, but we also learn to confront and overcome discomfort. This process of acclimating to the cold serves as a metaphor for facing life's challenges head-on, fostering resilience and self-confidence that can help us navigate our personal journeys with poise and determination.

THE FINAL COMPONENT of the Wim Hof Method is the cultivation of a strong, resilient mindset. Through meditation and visualization exercises, the method teaches us to train our minds to be more adaptable, focused, and tenacious. This mental fortitude is essential for living a life of purpose, as it enables us to persevere in the face of setbacks, maintain motivation, and remain optimistic even during trying times.

AS WE DELVE into the world of the Wim Hof Method, we'll explore the science and research that underpin its principles, demystifying the mechanisms through which breathwork, cold exposure, and mindset training contribute to our overall well-being. We'll examine real-life stories of individuals who have embraced the method, gaining insight into the transformative power it holds for those who commit to its practice. We'll also provide practical guidance on how to integrate the Wim Hof Method into your daily life, empowering you to embark on your own journey toward purpose, happiness, and fulfillment.

. . .

THE WIM HOF METHOD is more than a wellness technique; it is an invitation to embark on a journey of self-discovery and personal growth. Through the practice of breathwork, cold exposure, and mindset training, we can unlock our true potential, tap into our inner reservoirs of strength, and cultivate a sense of purpose that resonates deeply within us. As we embrace the method and experience its transformative effects, we not only improve our own well-being, but also inspire those around us to pursue their paths of self-improvement and growth.

THE JOURNEY to living a life of purpose and fulfillment is both a deeply personal and universal quest. It is a journey that demands courage, curiosity, and dedication, as we confront our fears, overcome our limitations, and embrace our unique strengths. The Wim Hof Method serves as a powerful ally in this pursuit, providing a roadmap and toolkit for personal transformation that transcends conventional wellness practices.

AS YOU DELVE into the pages of this book, you will uncover the secrets of the Wim Hof Method and learn to harness its power in your own life. You will discover the untapped potential within yourself, and find the courage to pursue your passions and dreams. This is more than a mere guide to a wellness technique; it is an invitation to awaken your spirit, challenge your limits, and embark on a lifelong journey of self-discovery and growth.

TOGETHER, we will traverse the landscape of the human spirit, exploring the depths of our resilience and the heights of our potential. Along the way, we will encounter inspiring stories of transformation, delve into the scientific foundations of the method, and learn practical strategies for integrating its principles into our daily lives. With each step, we will forge new connections with our inner selves and the world around us, cultivating a sense of purpose that fuels our dreams and enriches our lives.

1

DISCOVERING THE WIM HOF METHOD

A PATH TO EXTRAORDINARY HEALTH

Meet Wim Hof: The Ice Man

Let's dive into the frosty world of Wim Hof, the man who defied the laws of nature and transformed his life through cold exposure and controlled breathing. Known as the Ice Man, Wim Hof has dedicated his life to helping others unlock their potential and achieve optimal health, proving that the seemingly impossible is within reach. As we explore the life and achievements of this extraordinary individual, you'll discover how his unique method can revolutionize your life, too.

BORN in the Netherlands in 1959, Wim Hof's journey began with a simple curiosity that led him to experiment with icy waters. His connection to the cold started when he was just 17 years old, as he took his first plunge into a frozen pond. This experience ignited a spark within him, leading to a lifetime of exploration and discovery in the realms of mind and body.

THROUGHOUT HIS LIFE, Wim Hof continued to develop his unique approach to cold exposure and controlled breathing. Over the years, he has broken multiple world records, including climbing Mount Kilimanjaro and Everest wearing only shorts, swimming under ice, and completing a full marathon in the Namib Desert without drinking water. His incredible feats of endurance and mental strength have attracted the attention of both the media and the scientific community, further fueling the curiosity surrounding his method.

WIM HOF'S ability to withstand extreme cold and control his body's physiological responses can be attributed to his deep understanding and mastery of his own breath. Through a combination of cold exposure and controlled breathing, he has developed a method that enables individuals to tap into their innate power and enhance their physical and mental well-being. The Wim Hof Method has since gained popularity worldwide, attracting a diverse range of followers seeking to improve their health, boost their immune system, and achieve peak performance.

As you delve deeper into the life of Wim Hof and explore his groundbreaking method, you'll find that it's not just about facing the cold. It's also about embracing the power of the mind and harnessing its potential to overcome physical and mental barriers. Wim Hof believes that the mind, body, and soul are interconnected, and through the practice of his method, one can achieve a harmonious balance that leads to improved health and overall well-being.

It's essential to remember that Wim Hof's success isn't solely based on his exceptional abilities. Instead, he is driven by an unwavering determination to challenge conventional wisdom and push the boundaries of human potential. His passion for self-discovery and exploration has led him to develop a method that can truly benefit everyone, regardless of age or background.

The story of Wim Hof, the Ice Man, serves as a testament to the power of human will and resilience. By daring to push the limits and embrace the unknown, he has unlocked the door to a world of possibilities that awaits those willing to take the plunge. As we continue to explore the Wim Hof Method, we'll delve into the science behind this extraordinary practice, unraveling the mysteries that surround cold exposure and controlled breathing. In doing so, we'll discover how understanding the science behind the method can provide the foundation for you to embark on a transformative journey, ultimately enhancing your health and empowering you to achieve the seemingly impossible.

Understanding the Science Behind the Method

DELVE into the fascinating world of the science behind the Wim Hof Method, a revolutionary practice that has transformed countless lives by tapping into the body's natural potential. By understanding the underlying principles of this method, you'll be equipped with the knowledge to harness the power of cold exposure and controlled breathing, enabling you to overcome mental and physical barriers and reach new heights.

THE WIM HOF METHOD primarily revolves around two key elements: cold exposure and controlled breathing. Cold exposure works by stimulating the body's natural response to cold temperatures, causing a series of physiological changes. For instance, when the body is exposed to cold, blood vessels constrict, resulting in increased blood flow and circulation. This response has been shown to improve immune function, reduce inflammation, and enhance overall health.

MOREOVER, cold exposure activates the body's natural production of brown adipose tissue, also known as brown fat. Unlike white fat, which stores energy, brown fat generates heat and burns calories. Studies have found that individuals with higher levels of brown fat tend to have faster metabolisms, making it easier for them to maintain a healthy weight and reduce their risk of developing metabolic disorders.

CONTROLLED BREATHING, the second pillar of the Wim Hof Method, focuses on optimizing the body's oxygen levels to improve overall health and performance. By engaging in deep, rhythmic breathing, you can increase the amount of oxygen in your blood, which in turn enhances cellular respiration and energy production. This practice also stimulates the release of endorphins, promoting feelings of happiness and well-being while reducing stress and anxiety.

ONE OF THE most significant aspects of the Wim Hof Method is its impact on the autonomic nervous system, which regulates essential functions such as heart rate, digestion, and respiratory rate. Traditionally, it was believed that the autonomic nervous system could not be consciously controlled. However, Wim Hof's remarkable achievements and the subsequent scientific research have demonstrated that with the right techniques, individuals can indeed influence their autonomic nervous system.

A GROUNDBREAKING STUDY conducted by Radboud University in the Netherlands provided evidence supporting the benefits of the Wim Hof Method. Participants who practiced the method showed a significant increase in their ability to withstand cold temperatures and reported a decrease in inflammation markers. Furthermore, the study revealed that these individuals could voluntarily activate their sympathetic nervous system, a feat previously thought to be impossible.

WHILE THE WIM HOF METHOD is rooted in science, it's essential to recognize that it is not a one-size-fits-all solution. Each individual's response to the method may vary, and it's crucial to listen to your body and adapt the practice to your unique needs and limitations. By doing so, you'll be able to experience the full potential of this transformative method, ultimately leading to improved health, resilience, and performance.

AS WE CONTINUE to explore the Wim Hof Method, it's vital to address the myths and misconceptions that may arise. By debunking these misconceptions, we'll shed light on the true nature of the method and empower you to make informed decisions as you embark on your journey toward optimal health and well-being. So, buckle up and get ready to uncover the truth behind the Wim Hof Method, a practice that has the power to revolutionize your life and unlock your full potential.

Debunking Myths and Misconceptions

IT'S time to separate fact from fiction and debunk myths and misconceptions surrounding the Wim Hof Method. By dispelling these inaccuracies, you'll be better equipped to embrace the benefits of this transformative practice, empowering you to unlock your full potential and enhance your physical and mental well-being.

A COMMON MISCONCEPTION about the Wim Hof Method is that it's reserved for the fearless and the physically elite. The reality, however, is that this practice is accessible to anyone willing to step outside their comfort zone and explore their body's innate capabilities. While it's true that some individuals, such as Wim Hof himself, have taken the method to extreme levels, the core principles can be adapted to suit the needs and limitations of each individual.

ANOTHER MYTH IS that the Wim Hof Method is purely a cold exposure practice, with some believing that simply taking cold showers or ice baths is all that's required. Although cold exposure is a significant component of the method, controlled breathing and mindset training play equally important roles in achieving the desired outcomes. It's the synergy of these three elements that allows practitioners to reap the full benefits of the Wim Hof Method.

SOME SKEPTICS MAY ARGUE that the Wim Hof Method is nothing more than a placebo effect, with the power of belief driving the positive results. However, numerous scientific studies have validated the efficacy of the method, demonstrating its impact on the immune system, inflammation, and the autonomic nervous system. These findings provide substantial evidence that the Wim Hof Method goes beyond mere placebo and has a genuine effect on the body and mind.

IT'S ALSO worth addressing the misconception that practicing the Wim Hof Method is dangerous or risky. While there are inherent risks associated with cold exposure and breath-holding exercises, these can be minimized by following proper guidelines and listening to your body. It's crucial to build up your tolerance gradually and avoid pushing yourself beyond your limits. By doing so, you can safely harness the power of the Wim Hof Method without jeopardizing your health.

LASTLY, some people may believe that the Wim Hof Method is a cure-all solution to a wide range of health issues. While the method has been shown to improve various aspects of health, it should not be considered a substitute for medical advice or treatment. It's essential to view the Wim Hof Method as a complementary practice that can enhance your overall well-being and work in tandem with conventional medical care.

NOW THAT WE'VE dispelled these myths and misconceptions, it's time to dive deeper into the world of the Wim Hof Method and explore the myriad benefits it has to offer. In the upcoming section, we'll delve into the transformative effects of this practice on both your body and mind. From boosting your immune system to enhancing mental clarity, you'll soon discover how the Wim Hof Method can revolutionize your life and set you on a path towards optimal health and happiness. Get ready to embrace the power within you and unlock your full potential as we continue this exhilarating journey.

Embracing the Benefits: Physical and Mental Well-being

ONCE YOU UNDERSTAND the remarkable benefits of the Wim Hof Method and its impact on physical and mental well-being you might just think you uncovered a secret of the universe. By embracing this transformative practice, you'll unlock a world of possibilities, enhancing your overall health and empowering you to reach new heights in both your personal and professional life.

A CORNERSTONE of the Wim Hof Method's physical benefits lies in its ability to strengthen the immune system. Cold exposure and controlled breathing work in tandem to stimulate the body's natural defenses, making it more resilient to illness and infection. Studies have shown that individuals who practice the Wim Hof Method exhibit increased white blood cell production and reduced inflammatory markers, equipping them with a more robust immune response.

BEYOND IMMUNE FUNCTION, the Wim Hof Method has been found to improve cardiovascular health. By exposing the body to cold temperatures, blood vessels constrict and then dilate, promoting better circulation and oxygen delivery to vital organs. This process can lead to increased energy levels, reduced fatigue, and enhanced endurance, making it easier for practitioners to tackle daily tasks and challenges.

THE WIM HOF METHOD'S controlled breathing exercises also play a crucial role in physical well-being. By increasing oxygen levels in the bloodstream, these exercises promote optimal cellular function, facilitating more efficient energy production and helping the body perform at its best. This heightened state of oxygenation can also contribute to faster recovery from physical exertion and improved athletic performance.

. . .

In addition to its physical benefits, the Wim Hof Method boasts a host of mental health advantages. One of the most notable effects is its ability to alleviate stress and anxiety. The controlled breathing exercises help activate the parasympathetic nervous system, which is responsible for the body's relaxation response. By tapping into this calming state, practitioners can experience reduced stress levels, lower blood pressure, and a greater sense of overall well-being.

Moreover, the Wim Hof Method has been shown to enhance mental clarity and focus. The combination of cold exposure and controlled breathing exercises can increase the release of endorphins and other neurotransmitters, which are crucial for maintaining a positive mood and sharp mental acuity. This boost in cognitive function can lead to better decision-making, heightened creativity, and improved problem-solving skills.

The Wim Hof Method's impact on mental well-being also extends to fostering resilience and mental fortitude. By challenging the body and mind to overcome the discomfort of cold exposure, practitioners develop a more robust mindset, enabling them to face life's obstacles with greater courage and determination. This newfound sense of inner strength can translate to increased confidence and self-esteem, further fueling personal and professional growth.

As we continue to learn more about the wonders of the Wim Hof Method, we'll shift our focus to the power of oxygen and its role in our bodies. In the next section, we'll uncover the science behind controlled breathing and its profound effects on our physical and mental health. From optimizing energy production to promoting relaxation, prepare to be amazed by the incredible potential that lies within each breath.

2

BREATHING TO ENERGIZE
MASTERING THE WIM HOF BREATHING TECHNIQUE

The Power of Oxygen: How Breathing Affects Your Body

At the heart of the Wim Hof Method's effectiveness lies the incredible role of oxygen in our bodies. Oxygen is a vital component in the production of adenosine triphosphate (ATP), the primary source of cellular energy. With every breath we take, we fuel our cells with the necessary resources to perform countless tasks, from muscle contractions to brain activity.

WHEN WE PRACTICE CONTROLLED breathing exercises, like those found in the Wim Hof Method, we can optimize oxygen intake and enhance our body's ability to generate energy. By taking slow, deep breaths, we allow more oxygen to enter our bloodstream and reach our cells, leading to more efficient energy production and improved overall function.

IN ADDITION to its impact on energy levels, proper oxygenation can have profound effects on our mental health. Oxygen plays a crucial role in maintaining a healthy brain, as it helps regulate the production and release of neurotransmitters, such as serotonin and dopamine. These chemicals are essential for promoting a positive mood, reducing stress, and enhancing focus. By engaging in controlled breathing exercises, we can ensure our brain receives the optimal amount of oxygen it needs to function at its best.

ANOTHER FASCINATING ASPECT of oxygen's role in our bodies involves its connection to the autonomic nervous system. This system, responsible for regulating many of our body's automatic functions, is divided into two branches: the sympathetic nervous system (SNS) and the parasympathetic nervous system (PNS). The SNS is responsible for activating our "fight or flight" response during times of stress, while the PNS helps us enter a more relaxed, "rest and digest" state.

BREATHING IS something we do every day without giving it much thought. But what if I told you that the simple act of focusing on your breath could bring about a wide range of health benefits? The Wim Hof Method, a set of breathing exercises, is here to show you how.

THE WIM HOF METHOD revolves around controlled breathing exercises that aim to balance the parts of our nervous system responsible for rest and action. You see, our body's autonomic nervous system has two main parts: the sympathetic nervous system (SNS) and the parasympathetic nervous system (PNS). The SNS is in charge of our "fight or flight" response, while the PNS helps us "rest and digest." In our fast-paced world, it's common for the SNS to be overactive, leaving us feeling stressed and on edge.

THAT'S where the Wim Hof Method comes in. By focusing on slow, deep breaths, we can activate the PNS and tell our brain it's time to relax. The result? A whole host of positive changes in our body, like less anxiety, lower blood pressure, and better digestion.

YOU MIGHT BE WONDERING, "How exactly does the Wim Hof Method work?" Well, the process is simple but powerful. It involves taking a series of deep breaths in and then exhaling without forcing the air out. After doing this several times, you hold your breath on the last exhale for as long as you can. Finally, you take a big breath in and hold it for a short time before returning to normal breathing.

WHEN YOU PRACTICE these exercises regularly, you'll start to notice that your body and mind feel more balanced. For example, people who use the Wim Hof Method often report feeling calmer and more focused throughout the day. And because a relaxed mind is closely linked to a healthy body, many users also notice improvements in their physical well-being.

BUT THE BENEFITS don't stop there. The Wim Hof Method is also known to help with sleep. Having trouble falling asleep or staying asleep is often a result of an overactive SNS. By using the breathing exercises to activate the PNS, you can calm your body and mind, making it easier to drift off into a peaceful slumber.

THE WIM HOF METHOD can even support a stronger immune system. Studies have shown that regular practice can lead to a decrease in inflammation, which is a key factor in many health issues, including chronic pain and autoimmune diseases. By keeping inflammation in check, the Wim Hof Method can help your body stay healthy and better equipped to fight off illness.

THE BEAUTY of the Wim Hof Method is that it's accessible to everyone, regardless of age, fitness level, or experience with breathing exercises. All it takes is a commitment to practice and an openness to the transformative power of the breath.

AS YOU CONTINUE to use the Wim Hof Method, you may find that it becomes an essential part of your daily routine. Many people look forward to their breathing sessions as a way to center themselves and prepare for the day ahead or unwind after a long day.

THE IMPACT of the Wim Hof Method on overall well-being cannot be understated. By tapping into the power of controlled breathing, you can unlock a world of benefits that ripple out into every aspect of your life. From reduced stress and improved sleep to better digestion and a stronger immune system, the potential gains are vast and varied.

PERHAPS ONE OF the most intriguing aspects of the power of oxygen is its ability to boost our body's innate healing processes. When our cells have access to an optimal supply of oxygen, they can more effectively repair damaged tissues and fend off potential infections. This heightened state of healing can contribute to faster recovery from injuries, reduced inflammation, and a stronger immune system.

Step-by-Step Guide to the Wim Hof Breathing Technique

THE WIM HOF BREATHING TECHNIQUE revolves around three main components: deep inhales, passive exhales, and breath retention. Begin by finding a comfortable position, either sitting or lying down, where you can fully relax and focus on your breath. Ensure that you are in a safe environment, as the technique may cause lightheadedness.

ONCE SETTLED, initiate the process with a series of deep, diaphragmatic breaths. Inhale through your nose, filling your lungs to their maximum capacity. Visualize the air flowing down into your diaphragm, allowing your belly to expand outward. This deep breathing helps maximize oxygen intake and stimulate the body's natural relaxation response.

FOLLOWING EACH DEEP INHALE, let the air flow out of your lungs effortlessly through your mouth. Avoid forcefully exhaling or holding your breath. Instead, allow your body to release the air naturally, without any tension or strain. This passive exhale enables your body to release carbon dioxide and maintain a healthy balance of gases within your bloodstream.

CONTINUE the cycle of deep inhales and passive exhales for approximately 30 to 40 breaths, or until you start to feel a tingling sensation in your extremities. This sensation is a sign that your body is ready for the next phase: breath retention.

UPON COMPLETING YOUR FINAL EXHALE, pause and hold your breath for as long as you comfortably can. This breath retention phase allows your body to further absorb oxygen and release carbon dioxide, promoting a state of deep relaxation and enhanced focus. As you hold your breath, remain calm and composed, observing any sensations or thoughts that arise.

WHEN YOU FEEL the urge to breathe again, take one more deep inhale, filling your lungs completely. Hold this breath for approximately 15 seconds before releasing it slowly through your mouth. This final inhale and brief retention serve as a "recovery breath," allowing your body to re-establish its equilibrium.

REPEAT the entire process for two to four more rounds, or as long as you feel comfortable. With each cycle, you may find yourself able to hold your breath for longer periods, further enhancing the technique's benefits.

Tips for Proper Technique and Avoiding Common Mistakes

SELECTING an appropriate location is crucial to the success of your practice. Find a quiet, comfortable space free from distractions, ensuring you have ample room to breathe and stretch. Whether indoors or outdoors, the environment should encourage relaxation and focus, setting the stage for a productive session.

MAINTAINING proper posture is equally important, as it enables you to breathe deeply and efficiently. Regardless of whether you're sitting or lying down, ensure your spine is in a neutral position, with your head, neck, and shoulders relaxed. Avoid slouching, as this can restrict airflow and hinder the effectiveness of your practice.

WHILE THE WIM HOF BREATHING TECHNIQUE may be intense, it's essential to listen to your body and respect its limits. If you experience dizziness or lightheadedness, don't push yourself too hard. Instead, pause for a moment and resume the practice at a slower pace or with less intensity. Remember, your well-being should always come first.

CONSISTENCY IS the key to achieving lasting benefits from your breathing practice. Make a commitment to regular sessions, ideally setting aside time each day for focused practice. This consistency will allow you to develop and refine your technique while fostering a deeper connection with your breath.

ONE COMMON MISTAKE is holding the breath for too long, which can result in unnecessary strain and discomfort. Instead, aim for a comfortable duration that allows you to experience the benefits of breath retention without compromising your well-being. With time and practice, your ability to hold your breath will naturally improve.

TO MAXIMIZE the effectiveness of your breathing practice, synchronize it with other aspects of your daily routine, such as meditation or exercise. By integrating your practice into a holistic approach to well-being, you'll create a synergistic effect that amplifies the benefits of each individual component.

ANOTHER CRITICAL ASPECT TO consider is your mindset. Approach your breathing practice with a curious and open mind, free from judgment or expectation. This attitude will allow you to fully immerse yourself in the experience and gain deeper insights into your breath and its impact on your body and mind.

Tailoring Your Breathing Practice for Optimal Results

BEGIN by identifying your specific objectives and intentions for your breathing practice. Are you looking to reduce stress, boost energy levels, or improve focus and concentration? By clarifying your goals, you'll be better equipped to design a personalized practice that addresses your unique needs and aspirations.

IT'S essential to consider your individual preferences and lifestyle when designing your breathing practice. Factors such as your daily schedule, preferred practice environment, and physical limitations can all play a role in determining the most effective approach for you. By taking these factors into account, you'll create a practice that seamlessly integrates with your life and yields maximum results.

EXPERIMENTATION IS a crucial aspect of tailoring your breathing practice. Be open to trying different techniques and approaches, monitoring their impact on your body and mind. By paying close attention to how various practices affect you, you'll gain valuable insights that inform your ongoing customization process.

. . .

Incorporating complementary practices, such as yoga, meditation, or mindfulness, can further enhance the benefits of your breathing practice. By combining these disciplines, you'll create a synergistic effect that amplifies the advantages of each component while fostering a holistic approach to well-being.

Don't be afraid to make adjustments to the duration, intensity, and frequency of your practice as needed. Remember, your needs may change over time as your body and mind evolve. By staying attuned to your shifting requirements and adapting your practice accordingly, you'll maintain a dynamic and responsive routine that continues to serve you well.

It's also important to recognize that your breathing practice may require different approaches depending on your current physical and emotional state. For example, if you're feeling anxious or overwhelmed, you may benefit from a calming technique, such as diaphragmatic breathing. Conversely, if you're seeking to boost your energy levels or focus, a more invigorating practice, like the Wim Hof Breathing Technique, may be more suitable.

Remember that consistency is key to achieving lasting benefits from your breathing practice. Establish a regular practice schedule, setting aside dedicated time each day for focused sessions. By making your breathing practice a non-negotiable aspect of your daily routine, you'll foster the discipline and commitment necessary for long-term success.

Developing a deeper understanding of your breath and its impact on your body and mind will also aid in your customization efforts. By educating yourself on the science and mechanics of breathing, you'll be better equipped to make informed decisions about which techniques and approaches are best suited to your needs.

. . .

DON'T HESITATE to seek guidance and support from experienced practitioners or experts in the field of breathwork. By tapping into their knowledge and insights, you'll gain valuable perspective and inspiration that can help you refine your practice and overcome any challenges that may arise.

ONE OF THE most critical aspects of tailoring your practice is remaining open to change and evolution. As you progress on your journey, your needs and goals may shift, necessitating adjustments to your approach. By staying flexible and open-minded, you'll ensure that your practice continues to serve you well throughout every stage of your personal growth journey.

3

COLD EXPOSURE
UNLEASHING YOUR INNER WARRIOR

The Science of Cold Therapy: Boosting Your Immune System

Cold therapy, also known as cryotherapy, has long been recognized for its ability to reduce inflammation and improve circulation. When the body is exposed to cold temperatures, it activates a series of physiological responses that help regulate the immune system. These responses include increased white blood cell production, which plays a vital role in defending the body against infections and disease.

IN ADDITION to enhancing immune function, cold therapy has been shown to stimulate the release of endorphins, also known as "feel-good" hormones. This flood of endorphins can help improve mood, reduce stress, and increase overall feelings of well-being. By incorporating cold therapy into your wellness routine, you'll not only support your immune system but also promote emotional balance and resilience.

ANOTHER KEY BENEFIT of cold therapy lies in its ability to activate brown adipose tissue, also known as brown fat. Unlike white fat, which stores excess energy, brown fat generates heat and burns calories. By stimulating brown fat through cold exposure, you can boost your metabolism and support weight management.

AS YOU EXPLORE the science of cold therapy, it's important to remember that every individual is unique, and what works for one person may not work for another. Always listen to your body and consult with a healthcare professional before beginning any new health regimen, especially if you have existing medical conditions or concerns.

. . .

If you're new to cold therapy, start by learning about various techniques and approaches, such as cold showers, ice baths, and cryotherapy chambers. By familiarizing yourself with these methods, you'll be better equipped to determine which approach best aligns with your goals and preferences.

It's also helpful to educate yourself on the science behind cold therapy. By understanding the physiological mechanisms at play, you'll gain a deeper appreciation for the practice and its potential benefits. This knowledge will empower you to make informed decisions about your cold therapy routine and ensure that you're maximizing its positive impact on your immune system and overall health.

As you experiment with cold therapy, be prepared for some initial discomfort. However, it's essential to distinguish between discomfort and pain. While a certain level of discomfort is normal, it's crucial to listen to your body and never push yourself to the point of pain or injury.

Remember that consistency is key when it comes to reaping the benefits of cold therapy. Establish a regular practice schedule and commit to it, just as you would with any other wellness routine. Over time, your body will adapt to the cold, and you'll begin to notice improvements in your immune function, mood, and energy levels.

Now that you're equipped with a solid understanding of the science behind cold therapy, it's time to take the plunge and explore the world of gradual exposure. From cold showers to ice baths, you'll learn how to safely and effectively incorporate cold therapy into your daily routine. By taking a measured and mindful approach, you'll unlock the full potential of this powerful practice, bolstering your immune system and fostering a greater sense of well-being.

Gradual Exposure: From Cold Showers to Ice Baths

EMBRACE the chill and unlock the transformative power of cold therapy by taking a step-by-step journey from cold showers to ice baths. Gradual exposure to the cold is the key to unlocking the full potential of this powerful practice, paving the way for a healthier and more resilient version of yourself.

STARTING with cold showers is a great way to ease into cold therapy. The simplicity and accessibility of this method make it an ideal entry point for those new to the practice. To begin, try ending your regular shower with a 30-second burst of cold water. As your body adapts, you can gradually increase the duration and intensity of the cold exposure, eventually working up to a full cold shower.

AS YOU PROGRESS with cold showers, you'll likely begin to notice improvements in your mood, energy levels, and overall well-being. These positive changes are a testament to the power of gradual exposure and will serve as a source of motivation as you continue to challenge yourself.

WHEN YOU'RE ready to take your cold therapy practice to the next level, consider exploring the world of ice baths. This more intense form of cold exposure offers a range of benefits, including enhanced recovery, reduced inflammation, and improved immune function. However, it's important to approach ice baths with caution and respect, as the extreme temperatures involved can pose risks if not properly managed.

. . .

BEFORE DIVING INTO AN ICE BATH, it's essential to prepare both physically and mentally. Begin by taking slow, deep breaths to calm your mind and center your focus. This mindful approach will help you maintain control and presence throughout the experience.

WHEN YOU'RE ready to immerse yourself in the ice bath, do so slowly and mindfully. Remember that your body will naturally react to the cold with an initial shock response, characterized by rapid breathing and an increased heart rate. Focus on your breath and allow yourself to relax into the experience, acknowledging the discomfort without allowing it to overwhelm you.

AS YOU BECOME MORE comfortable with ice baths, you can experiment with various techniques and durations to find what works best for you. Some people prefer shorter, more intense sessions, while others may opt for longer, more moderate exposure. The key is to listen to your body and find the balance that maximizes the benefits without causing undue stress or strain.

THROUGHOUT YOUR COLD THERAPY JOURNEY, it's crucial to remember that consistency is key. Establish a regular practice schedule and commit to it, just as you would with any other wellness routine. By doing so, you'll continue to unlock the full potential of cold therapy, reaping the rewards of improved immune function, enhanced mood, and increased resilience.

AS YOU VENTURE FURTHER into the invigorating world of cold therapy, it's important to prioritize safety and best practices. Whether you're a seasoned ice bath enthusiast or just beginning your journey, staying informed and mindful of the risks and precautions associated with cold exposure will ensure that you're able to safely and effectively reap the benefits of this powerful practice.

. . .

IN THE UPCOMING SECTION, we'll delve deeper into the safety precautions and best practices that are essential for a successful and enjoyable cold therapy experience.

Safety Precautions and Best Practices

EMBARKING on the cold therapy journey can be invigorating and transformative, but it's essential to prioritize safety and adhere to best practices to ensure a rewarding experience. In this section, we'll explore the precautions and guidelines you should follow to make the most of your cold therapy practice while minimizing risk.

ONE OF THE fundamental principles of safe cold therapy is to listen to your body. While it's natural to experience discomfort during cold exposure, it's crucial to differentiate between manageable sensations and those that signal potential harm. If you ever feel lightheaded, dizzy, or experience intense pain, it's important to end the session immediately and warm up.

WHILE ENGAGING IN COLD THERAPY, maintaining a calm and focused mindset is vital. Before each session, take a moment to center yourself and practice deep, controlled breathing. This mental preparation will help you stay present and aware of your body's signals during the cold exposure, allowing you to respond effectively to any sensations or signs of distress.

WHEN YOU'RE ready to progress from cold showers to ice baths, be cautious and gradual in your approach. Start by immersing only your lower body and gradually work up to full immersion over time. This slow progression will help your body acclimate to the extreme temperatures and minimize the risk of adverse reactions.

ANOTHER ESSENTIAL ASPECT of cold therapy safety is understanding the importance of duration. While longer cold exposure sessions can offer increased benefits, it's crucial to strike a balance between maximizing gains and avoiding overexposure. As a general guideline, aim for sessions lasting between 2-10 minutes, but always defer to your body's feedback and adjust accordingly.

A CRUCIAL CONSIDERATION in cold therapy is the prevention of hypothermia. Make sure to monitor the temperature of your ice baths, and never let the water temperature drop below 50°F (10°C). Additionally, ensure that you have a way to rewarm your body quickly after each session, such as a warm blanket or a heated room.

IT'S ALSO important to be mindful of the environment in which you practice cold therapy. Ensure that the space is free of hazards, such as slippery surfaces or sharp objects, and always have a support system in place. This could be a buddy who joins you in the cold therapy session or someone who remains close by to offer assistance if needed.

REMEMBER that consistency is key when it comes to cold therapy. Establishing a regular routine and sticking to it will help you safely progress and maximize the benefits of this powerful practice. However, if you ever feel unwell or suspect that you may be coming down with an illness, it's best to pause your cold therapy practice until you recover.

AS YOU CONTINUE to hone your cold therapy skills, it's essential to track your progress and celebrate your milestones. In the next section, we'll delve into methods for monitoring your growth and acknowledging your accomplishments, fostering a sense of pride and motivation that will propel you further on your cold therapy journey.

BY KEEPING these safety precautions and best practices in mind, you'll be well-equipped to explore the transformative world of cold therapy with confidence and assurance. As you progress, you'll unlock the full potential of this powerful practice, boosting your immune system, enhancing your well-being, and discovering new depths of resilience and strength.

Tracking Progress and Celebrating Milestones

TRACKING progress and celebrating milestones is more than just a feel-good exercise—it's a vital component in the journey to growing your business and achieving your dreams. In this section, we'll explore the importance of monitoring your growth, acknowledging your accomplishments, and the various techniques that can help you stay motivated and focused on your goals.

ONE POWERFUL WAY TO track your progress is by keeping a detailed record of your achievements and challenges. A dedicated journal, spreadsheet, or digital app can serve as a valuable tool for logging your experiences and reflecting on your growth. By consistently documenting your journey, you'll be better equipped to identify areas for improvement and make informed decisions about the direction of your business.

BUT TRACKING progress doesn't have to be all about numbers and metrics. It's also essential to recognize the personal growth and insights you gain along the way. Pay attention to the lessons you learn, the relationships you build, and the obstacles you overcome. These intangible experiences are just as important as the quantifiable markers of success.

IN ADDITION to monitoring your progress, celebrating milestones is crucial in maintaining motivation and a positive mindset. When you reach a significant goal or complete a challenging project, take the time to acknowledge your hard work and dedication. Whether it's a small victory or a major breakthrough, every accomplishment deserves recognition.

CELEBRATIONS CAN BE AS simple or elaborate as you choose. You might want to share your success with friends or colleagues, treat yourself to a special indulgence, or simply take a moment to reflect on your journey so far. The key is to find a way to honor your achievements and reaffirm your commitment to your goals.

ANOTHER POWERFUL MOTIVATOR is sharing your journey with others. Joining a community or networking group can provide invaluable support and encouragement, as well as the opportunity to learn from the experiences of others. Connecting with like-minded individuals who share your passion and drive can help you stay focused and inspired on your path to success.

AS YOU TRACK your progress and celebrate milestones, don't forget to periodically reassess your goals and aspirations. The world of business is dynamic and ever-changing, and it's crucial to remain adaptable and open to new opportunities. By regularly evaluating your objectives and adjusting your course as needed, you'll ensure that you're always moving forward with purpose and intention.

IN THE PURSUIT OF SUCCESS, it's essential to recognize the intrinsic connection between your mind and body. As we transition to the next topic, we'll delve deeper into this profound relationship and explore how nurturing this connection can enhance your overall well-being and propel you towards your goals.

BY EMBRACING the practice of tracking progress and celebrating milestones, you'll not only gain valuable insights into your journey but also foster a sense of motivation and pride that will fuel your continued growth. Remember, every step forward brings you closer to achieving your dreams and unlocking your full potential. So, keep your eyes on the horizon, celebrate your achievements, and get ready to embrace the transformative power of understanding the connection between your mind and body.

4

MINDFULNESS AND MEDITATION
ENHANCING FOCUS AND CLARITY

Understanding the Connection between Mind and Body

Unlocking the powerful synergy between mind and body can be a game changer for people seeking to boost their performance, resilience, and overall well-being. In this section, we'll explore the intricate relationship between our thoughts, emotions, and physical health, and how nurturing this connection can propel your business to new heights.

THE MIND-BODY CONNECTION is rooted in the idea that our mental and emotional states can have a profound impact on our physical well-being. Stress, anxiety, and negative emotions can manifest in a myriad of physical symptoms, such as headaches, muscle tension, and even chronic illnesses. Conversely, positive thoughts and emotions can contribute to improved health, increased energy, and a heightened sense of vitality.

TO TRULY HARNESS the power of the mind-body connection, it's essential to develop a heightened awareness of your thoughts and emotions. By tuning into your inner landscape, you can begin to identify patterns and triggers that may be adversely affecting your physical health. Armed with this knowledge, you can take proactive steps to minimize stress, foster positive emotions, and create an environment that supports optimal well-being.

ONE POWERFUL TECHNIQUE for strengthening the mind-body connection is the practice of mindfulness. By cultivating an attitude of non-judgmental awareness, you can develop a deeper understanding of the interplay between your thoughts, emotions, and physical sensations. This heightened self-awareness can lead to improved stress management, increased emotional resilience, and a greater sense of balance and harmony in both your personal and professional life.

. . .

IN ADDITION TO MINDFULNESS, regular physical activity is a crucial component in fostering a healthy mind-body connection. Exercise has been shown to alleviate stress, boost mood, and improve cognitive function, making it a vital tool for entrepreneurs seeking to maintain peak performance. By integrating regular physical activity into your daily routine, you'll be better equipped to handle the challenges and demands of your business with clarity, focus, and resilience.

ANOTHER IMPORTANT ASPECT of the mind-body connection is the role of nutrition in supporting both mental and physical health. A balanced, nutrient-dense diet can contribute to increased energy levels, improved cognitive function, and a stronger immune system. By nourishing your body with the fuel it needs, you'll also be supporting the optimal function of your mind, setting the stage for continued success in your business endeavors.

REST AND RELAXATION also play a crucial role in nurturing the mind-body connection. Adequate sleep and intentional downtime are essential for maintaining physical health and mental clarity. By prioritizing self-care and giving your body the rest it needs, you'll be better prepared to face the challenges of entrepreneurship with renewed energy and enthusiasm.

AS WE MOVE FORWARD to the next topic, we'll delve into the practical aspects of integrating mindfulness practices into your daily routine. By incorporating these techniques, you'll be well on your way to cultivating a strong mind-body connection that will serve as a powerful foundation for continued growth and success.

IN CONCLUSION, understanding the connection between your mind and body is a vital aspect of achieving your goals and growing your business. By nurturing this relationship through mindfulness, exercise, nutrition, and rest, you'll be better equipped to handle the challenges and opportunities that come your way. So, embrace the power of the mind-body connection and get ready to experience the transformative benefits of integrating mindfulness practices into your daily routine.

Integrating Mindfulness Practices into Your Daily Routine

INCORPORATING mindfulness practices into your daily routine can be a powerful catalyst for personal growth and professional success. As we embark on this journey, you'll discover actionable strategies for weaving mindfulness into the fabric of your everyday life, enhancing your mental clarity, emotional resilience, and overall well-being.

A FUNDAMENTAL ASPECT of mindfulness is developing a consistent meditation practice. Even just a few minutes of meditation each day can yield profound benefits, including reduced stress, improved focus, and heightened self-awareness. To begin, choose a quiet space where you can sit comfortably and free of distractions. Focus on your breath, allowing your thoughts and emotions to come and go without judgment. With practice, you'll find that meditation becomes a natural and enjoyable part of your daily routine.

MINDFUL BREATHING EXERCISES can also be integrated into your day, providing a quick and effective way to center yourself amidst the hustle and bustle of your professional life. When you find yourself feeling overwhelmed or stressed, take a moment to pause and breathe deeply, focusing your attention on the sensations of your breath as it moves in and out of your body. This simple practice can bring you back to the present moment, enabling you to respond to challenges with greater clarity and composure.

ANOTHER POWERFUL MINDFULNESS technique is the body scan, which involves directing your attention to different parts of your body, noticing any sensations or tension that may be present. This practice can be done while sitting, lying down, or even standing, making it an adaptable addition to your daily routine. Regular body scans can enhance your mind-body connection, promoting relaxation and helping to release tension that may be hindering your productivity and well-being.

IN ADDITION to formal mindfulness practices, there are countless opportunities to incorporate mindfulness into everyday activities. Simple tasks like washing dishes, walking, or even brushing your teeth can become opportunities for present-moment awareness. By fully engaging with these activities, rather than letting your mind wander, you'll cultivate a deeper sense of connection with the present moment and enhance your overall quality of life.

DEVELOPING mindful communication skills is another valuable way to integrate mindfulness into your daily routine. By actively listening, maintaining eye contact, and responding thoughtfully, you'll foster more meaningful connections with colleagues, clients, and loved ones. Mindful communication can lead to improved collaboration, increased empathy, and greater emotional intelligence – all essential qualities.

A CONSISTENT GRATITUDE practice can also be a transformative component of your mindfulness journey. By taking time each day to reflect on the things you're grateful for, you'll nurture a more positive outlook, which can contribute to increased motivation and resilience in the face of challenges. Consider keeping a gratitude journal, or simply pause throughout the day to acknowledge the good things in your life.

AS WE TRANSITION to the next topic, we'll explore the powerful techniques of visualization and affirmations. By combining these strategies with your daily mindfulness practices, you'll create a potent formula for personal and professional growth.

IN CONCLUSION, integrating mindfulness practices into your daily routine is a powerful strategy for enhancing your mental clarity, emotional resilience, and overall well-being. As you begin to weave these techniques into the fabric of your everyday life, you'll discover a newfound sense of balance, focus, and purpose – essential ingredients for achieving your goals and growing your business. So, embark on this transformative journey and unlock the power of mindfulness to elevate your life and your entrepreneurial endeavors.

Harnessing the Power of Visualization and Affirmations

UNLOCKING the potential of visualization and affirmations can elevate your personal and professional life, empowering you to create the reality you desire. In this section, we'll delve into the art of crafting vivid mental images and positive self-talk, equipping you with the tools needed to overcome obstacles and manifest your goals.

VISUALIZATION IS a potent technique that involves creating mental images of the experiences and outcomes you wish to attract. It's rooted in the understanding that our thoughts have the power to shape our reality, and by focusing on our desired outcomes, we can attract them into existence. To practice visualization, find a quiet space where you can close your eyes and picture yourself achieving your goals. Immerse yourself in the scene, engaging all your senses to make the experience as vivid and realistic as possible. By regularly visualizing your success, you'll program your subconscious mind to believe in your potential, thereby increasing your motivation and confidence.

IN ADDITION TO VISUALIZATION, affirmations are powerful tools for reprogramming your mind and cultivating a positive mindset. Affirmations are positive, present-tense statements that reflect the beliefs and attitudes you wish to embody. By repeating these phrases, you can overwrite negative thought patterns and create a more empowering inner narrative. To create effective affirmations, choose statements that resonate with you and evoke strong emotions. For instance, instead of saying, "I will be successful," try, "I am a confident, capable entrepreneur who achieves remarkable results."

FOR MAXIMUM IMPACT, combine visualization and affirmations into a daily practice. Dedicate time each morning or evening to visualize your desired outcomes while repeating your chosen affirmations. As you engage in this practice, you'll notice a shift in your mindset, leading to increased self-belief and a heightened sense of purpose.

CONSISTENCY IS key when it comes to harnessing the power of visualization and affirmations. The more you practice these techniques, the more ingrained they will become in your subconscious mind, and the greater impact they will have on your life. Establishing a daily routine for your visualization and affirmation practice will help solidify these habits, making them a natural and enjoyable part of your personal growth journey.

. . .

WHILE VISUALIZATION and affirmations can be practiced individually, incorporating them into your existing mindfulness and meditation routine can amplify their effects. By combining these techniques, you create a holistic approach to personal development that addresses your thoughts, emotions, and physical sensations, fostering a deeper sense of self-awareness and inner harmony.

AS YOU BEGIN to master the art of visualization and affirmations, be patient with yourself and trust the process. It may take time to see tangible results, but rest assured that each practice session is contributing to your growth and setting the foundation for future success. Celebrate your progress, no matter how small, and remember that transformation is an ongoing journey.

AS WE VENTURE into the next topic, "Exploring Meditation Techniques for Deeper Connection," we'll delve into powerful practices that can enhance your visualization and affirmation routine. By integrating these techniques, you'll create a comprehensive approach to personal and professional growth, allowing you to connect more deeply with yourself and the world around you.

Exploring Meditation Techniques for Deeper Connection

DIVING into the world of meditation can open the door to a deeper connection with yourself and the world around you. By exploring various meditation techniques, you'll unlock the benefits of inner tranquility, clarity, and heightened awareness, all of which can enhance your overall well-being.

. . .

MEDITATION IS an ancient practice that involves focusing the mind to achieve a state of relaxation and heightened awareness. There are countless techniques to choose from, each offering its unique approach and benefits. By experimenting with different methods, you'll find the one that resonates most with you and your goals.

A POPULAR MEDITATION technique is mindfulness meditation, which emphasizes cultivating awareness and acceptance of the present moment. This practice encourages you to focus on your breath, bodily sensations, or thoughts without judgment, helping to quiet the mind and develop a greater sense of self-awareness.

ANOTHER POWERFUL METHOD TO explore is loving-kindness meditation, also known as Metta meditation. This technique involves directing positive thoughts and intentions towards yourself, others, and the world at large. By cultivating feelings of love, compassion, and goodwill, you'll nurture a deeper connection with others and enhance your emotional well-being.

FOR THOSE SEEKING A MORE structured approach, guided meditation may be an ideal choice. In guided meditation, an experienced teacher leads you through a series of instructions, helping you to focus your mind and enter a state of relaxation. This method is especially beneficial for beginners, as it provides a clear framework and support system to help you develop your meditation practice.

ANOTHER MEDITATION technique worth exploring is transcendental meditation, which involves the repetition of a specific mantra to quiet the mind and induce a state of deep relaxation. This practice has been widely studied and is known for its stress-reducing effects, making it a valuable tool for enhancing mental and emotional well-being.

. . .

As you embark on your meditation journey, remember that consistency is key. It's essential to commit to regular practice, even if it's just a few minutes each day. Over time, you'll notice improvements in your focus, emotional regulation, and overall well-being, making the effort well worth it.

Additionally, it's crucial to maintain an open mind and a sense of curiosity as you explore different meditation techniques. Each method has its unique benefits and may resonate differently with you at various stages of your life. By embracing this spirit of exploration, you'll create a meditation practice that is truly your own.

As we continue on this transformative journey, we'll soon explore the intriguing world of the Wim Hof Method. This powerful practice combines meditation, breathing exercises, and cold exposure to enhance mental and physical well-being. Get ready to dive into the realm of the "Iceman" and discover how to create your personalized Wim Hof routine.

Exploring various meditation techniques is a powerful way to cultivate a deeper connection with yourself and the world around you. Whether you choose mindfulness, loving-kindness, guided, or transcendental meditation, commit to regular practice and maintain an open mind to unlock the full potential of this transformative journey.

5

UNITING THE PILLARS
COMBINING BREATHING, COLD, AND MINDFULNESS

Creating Your Personalized Wim Hof Routine

Unlocking the full potential of the Wim Hof Method starts with crafting a personalized routine that fits seamlessly into your life. By tailoring the practice to your unique needs and schedule, you can make the most of this powerful technique and reap the numerous benefits it has to offer.

DEVELOPING A PERSONALIZED Wim Hof routine begins with understanding the three main components of the method: breathing, cold exposure, and commitment. The breathing exercises help to activate your parasympathetic nervous system, promoting relaxation and reducing stress. Cold exposure, on the other hand, trains your body to adapt to challenging conditions and boosts your immune system. Lastly, commitment is crucial for reaping the full benefits of the method, as consistent practice is key.

WHEN CRAFTING YOUR ROUTINE, it's essential to consider your current lifestyle and limitations. For instance, if you're a busy student or working professional, you might find it more convenient to practice the breathing exercises in the morning before your day begins or in the evening to unwind. Similarly, if you live in a warm climate, you could opt for cold showers or ice baths to experience the benefits of cold exposure.

THE FLEXIBILITY of the Wim Hof Method allows for adaptation to various fitness levels and personal preferences. For example, you can adjust the duration and intensity of the breathing exercises to suit your comfort level. As you become more familiar with the technique, you can gradually increase the intensity or duration to continue challenging yourself and enhancing the benefits.

. . .

To MAXIMIZE your progress and maintain motivation, it's a good idea to track your experiences and improvements. You can keep a journal or use an app to record the length of your breathing exercises, the duration of your cold exposure, and any noticeable changes in your well-being. This way, you'll be able to celebrate your achievements and stay committed to your practice.

IT'S important to remember that the Wim Hof Method is not a one-size-fits-all solution. Be patient with yourself as you explore the different aspects of the practice and find what works best for you. By listening to your body and adjusting your routine accordingly, you can create a sustainable and enjoyable practice that supports your overall health and well-being.

ONE OF THE most rewarding aspects of the Wim Hof Method is the opportunity to connect with a supportive community of likeminded individuals. By sharing your experiences and learning from others, you can gain valuable insights and encouragement to help you stay committed to your practice. There are numerous online forums, social media groups, and local meetups where you can connect with fellow practitioners and exchange tips and advice.

As YOU CONTINUE to develop and refine your personalized Wim Hof routine, it's essential to keep sight of the importance of consistency and commitment. The true power of the method lies in its ability to transform your life when practiced regularly and wholeheartedly. By staying dedicated to your practice and embracing the journey, you can unlock the full potential of the Wim Hof Method and experience a profound shift in your overall happiness and fulfillment.

The Importance of Consistency and Commitment

. . .

CONSISTENCY AND COMMITMENT are the cornerstones of personal growth and success, no matter what goal you're pursuing. By embracing these two principles, you lay the groundwork for lasting change and unlock the full potential of any endeavor, including the transformative power of the Wim Hof Method.

CONSISTENCY IS vital because it helps you develop good habits, which in turn lead to lasting results. When you practice the Wim Hof Method or any other self-improvement technique consistently, you're essentially training your mind and body to adapt to the new routine. Over time, this consistent practice allows you to reap the benefits of your efforts more effectively, as your body becomes more efficient at performing the exercises and adapting to the new stimuli.

THINK of consistency as the building blocks of success. Each time you practice, you add another block to the foundation, strengthening your resolve and increasing your chances of achieving your goals. By staying consistent, you also allow yourself to track your progress more accurately and make adjustments as needed, ensuring that you're always moving forward.

COMMITMENT, on the other hand, is the fuel that drives your consistency. It's the dedication and determination to see your goals through to the end, even when faced with setbacks or challenges. By committing wholeheartedly to your practice, you create an unshakable belief in your ability to succeed, which can propel you through moments of doubt or difficulty.

ONE WAY TO strengthen your commitment is to remind yourself of your "why"—the underlying reasons for wanting to pursue a particular goal. Your "why" could be anything from improving your health to boosting your self-confidence. By connecting with this deeper motivation, you'll find it easier to stay committed and push through any obstacles that may arise.

ACCOUNTABILITY CAN ALSO PLAY a crucial role in maintaining consistency and commitment. By sharing your goals with others or joining a community of like-minded individuals, you'll be more likely to stick to your plan and stay motivated. Moreover, you'll have access to a wealth of knowledge and support, which can make all the difference when faced with challenges.

IT'S important to note that consistency and commitment don't mean perfection. It's normal to encounter setbacks or have days when you struggle to maintain your routine. The key is to recognize these moments as opportunities for growth and learning, rather than letting them derail your progress entirely. By adopting a growth mindset and staying focused on your goals, you can bounce back from setbacks and continue moving forward.

AS YOU PROGRESS on your journey, you may also encounter plateaus or face new challenges. These moments can test your consistency and commitment, but they also offer valuable opportunities for growth and adaptation. By staying dedicated to your practice and embracing change, you can continue to evolve and unlock new levels of success.

AS YOU DELVE DEEPER into the world of personal growth and transformation, remember that consistency and commitment are the keys to unlocking your full potential. By staying dedicated to your practice and adapting to challenges, you'll be well-equipped to overcome plateaus and achieve lasting change. Embrace the journey, and watch as your newfound consistency and commitment open doors to a world of possibilities.

Overcoming Plateaus and Adapting to Challenges

OVERCOMING PLATEAUS and adapting to challenges are essential skills for anyone seeking personal growth and lasting change. By learning to navigate these inevitable bumps in the road, you'll be better equipped to stay committed, maintain your progress, and ultimately achieve your goals.

PLATEAUS ARE a natural part of any personal development journey. They represent a temporary stagnation in progress, often resulting from the body and mind adapting to a new routine. The key to overcoming plateaus is recognizing them as a sign that it's time to shake things up and introduce new strategies or techniques to keep yourself challenged and engaged.

ONE EFFECTIVE WAY TO break through a plateau is to vary your approach. If you've been practicing the Wim Hof Method consistently, for example, consider incorporating different breathing exercises, varying the duration of your cold exposure, or exploring other complementary practices, such as yoga or meditation. By introducing new stimuli, you encourage your body and mind to continue growing and adapting.

ANOTHER CRUCIAL ASPECT of overcoming plateaus is learning to embrace challenges. Challenges are an inevitable part of any journey, and they often serve as valuable opportunities for growth and self-discovery. When faced with a challenge, rather than seeing it as a setback, view it as a chance to learn, adapt, and become stronger.

TO SUCCESSFULLY NAVIGATE CHALLENGES, it's essential to develop resilience and a growth mindset. Resilience is the ability to bounce back from setbacks and persevere in the face of adversity. You can cultivate resilience by focusing on your strengths, maintaining a positive outlook, and seeking out support from others. A growth mindset, on the other hand, involves embracing the idea that your abilities and intelligence can be developed through dedication and effort. By adopting a growth mindset, you'll be more likely to see challenges as opportunities to learn and improve, rather than insurmountable obstacles.

ONE POWERFUL STRATEGY for adapting to challenges is to break them down into smaller, more manageable steps. By taking a step-by-step approach, you can maintain your momentum and avoid becoming overwhelmed. Remember that progress is often slow and steady, and even small victories can lead to significant long-term gains.

IT'S ALSO important to practice self-compassion and patience when faced with plateaus and challenges. Personal growth is a life-long journey, and there will inevitably be ups and downs along the way. By treating yourself with kindness and understanding, you'll be better equipped to stay committed and maintain a positive attitude, even when the going gets tough.

Nurturing a Supportive Community and Accountability System

BUILDING a supportive community and an accountability system can be a game-changer in your journey towards personal growth and success. Connecting with like-minded individuals who share your goals and aspirations can provide encouragement, motivation, and valuable insights. With the right group of people by your side, you'll find it much easier to stay committed to your path and overcome any obstacles that may come your way.

. . .

ONE KEY ASPECT of nurturing a supportive community is being intentional about the relationships you form. Seek out those who inspire you and share your core values. This can be done by attending events, joining clubs, or participating in online forums related to your interests. As you engage with others, be open to learning from their experiences and perspectives. Remember, it's not just about what they can offer you, but also how you can contribute to their growth and well-being.

ANOTHER IMPORTANT ELEMENT of creating an accountability system is setting clear expectations and goals. Communicate your intentions with your support network and encourage them to share their objectives as well. This mutual understanding of each other's aspirations helps foster a sense of shared purpose and responsibility. Together, you can brainstorm strategies for overcoming challenges and celebrate your victories.

FREQUENT CHECK-INS with your community members play a crucial role in maintaining accountability. Establish a regular schedule for catching up and discussing progress, either in person or through digital platforms. These meetings can serve as a valuable opportunity for feedback, encouragement, and the exchange of ideas. Be honest about your setbacks and achievements, and be open to receiving constructive criticism.

AN ESSENTIAL PART of any supportive community is cultivating trust and empathy. Make an effort to truly understand and empathize with the challenges faced by your fellow community members. Offer your support and encouragement without judgment, and be receptive to their insights and suggestions. By fostering an environment of genuine care and understanding, you can help each other grow and develop resilience in the face of adversity.

. . .

IN ADDITION to nurturing strong connections with others, it's important to prioritize self-reflection and personal growth. Regularly assess your progress and be honest with yourself about areas that need improvement. Utilize the insights and advice from your support network to refine your strategies and approach. This ongoing process of learning and adaptation is vital for overcoming plateaus and embracing new challenges.

ONE WAY TO enhance your support system is by incorporating mentorship and coaching. Reach out to individuals who have achieved success in your area of interest and ask for guidance. Their wisdom and experience can provide invaluable direction and support. Be open to learning from their successes and failures, and use their insights to inform your own journey.

BUILDING a strong community and accountability system requires effort, dedication, and commitment. However, the rewards of having a network of supportive individuals who share your goals and aspirations are well worth the investment. Together, you can overcome obstacles, achieve your dreams, and grow both personally and professionally. By fostering meaningful connections, setting clear expectations, and prioritizing personal growth, you'll be well-equipped to face any challenges that come your way and emerge stronger and more resilient.

6

NUTRITION FOR OPTIMAL PERFORMANCE

FUELING YOUR WIM HOF JOURNEY

The Connection between Diet and the Wim Hof Method

Unlocking the synergy between diet and the Wim Hof Method can supercharge your journey to improved health and well-being. By optimizing your nutritional intake alongside practicing the Wim Hof Method, you can enhance your mental clarity, physical endurance, and overall vitality. Let's delve into the connection between these two powerful forces and explore how they can work together for your benefit.

WHEN PRACTICING the Wim Hof Method, which involves cold exposure, breathing exercises, and meditation, you're putting your body through a unique set of challenges. It's crucial to fuel your body with the right nutrients to support these demands. A well-balanced diet rich in whole foods, such as fruits, vegetables, lean proteins, and healthy fats, provides the energy and nutrients necessary for optimal performance.

COLD EXPOSURE, one of the key components of the Wim Hof Method, has been shown to increase the body's production of brown adipose tissue, or brown fat. This unique type of fat is metabolically active and helps generate heat to keep you warm during cold exposure. Consuming a diet that supports brown fat activation, such as one rich in omega-3 fatty acids found in fatty fish, chia seeds, and walnuts, can further enhance the benefits of cold therapy.

THE BREATHING EXERCISES associated with the Wim Hof Method require a strong respiratory system. Consuming antioxidant-rich foods, like colorful fruits and vegetables, can help protect your lungs from oxidative stress and support their function during these exercises. Vitamin C and other antioxidants found in these foods can also contribute to a stronger immune system, which is one of the primary goals of the Wim Hof Method.

MEDITATION, another essential aspect of the Wim Hof Method, aims to improve mental clarity and focus. Your diet can have a profound impact on your cognitive function and ability to maintain concentration during meditation. Foods that are high in brain-boosting nutrients, such as leafy greens, blueberries, and walnuts, can help enhance mental performance.

HYDRATION IS ALSO crucial for the optimal functioning of both the Wim Hof Method and your overall well-being. Drinking enough water throughout the day can improve your energy levels, support detoxification, and keep your body operating at its best. Adequate hydration can also enhance the effectiveness of your breathing exercises by maintaining proper lung function.

WHILE THE WIM HOF METHOD can provide numerous benefits on its own, it's essential to remember that it's just one part of a holistic approach to health and wellness. A diet that complements the demands of this unique method will help you maximize its potential and better support your body throughout the process.

FINDING the right balance between diet and the Wim Hof Method may take some experimentation and adjustment. It's essential to listen to your body's signals and be open to making changes as needed. As you continue to refine your approach, you'll be better equipped to harness the full power of the Wim Hof Method and unlock a new level of well-being.

BY UNDERSTANDING the connection between diet and the Wim Hof Method, you can optimize your nutritional choices to support your body's unique needs. This powerful combination can lead to improved physical and mental health, increased resilience, and a greater sense of balance and vitality in your daily life. Embrace the synergy between these two transformative forces, and you'll be well on your way to unlocking your full potential.

Selecting Nutrient-Dense Foods for Energy and Recovery

FUELING your body with nutrient-dense foods is a game-changer for boosting energy levels and accelerating recovery. By focusing on foods that deliver the most nutritional bang for your buck, you can optimize your diet to support your active lifestyle and overall well-being. Let's explore the world of nutrient-dense foods and learn how to choose the best options for your needs.

ONE OF THE essential elements of nutrient-dense foods is their ability to provide a wealth of vitamins, minerals, and other nutrients without packing on excess calories. Foods like leafy greens, cruciferous vegetables, and brightly colored fruits are packed with essential nutrients that support energy production and recovery. For instance, spinach and kale are rich in iron, a crucial component of hemoglobin, which helps transport oxygen to your muscles, while berries are loaded with antioxidants that can help reduce inflammation and support recovery.

PROTEIN IS another vital nutrient for energy and recovery. Active individuals need ample protein to support muscle repair and growth, as well as to maintain a healthy immune system. Nutrient-dense protein sources include lean meats, fish, eggs, and plant-based options like beans, lentils, and tofu. These foods not only provide essential amino acids but also deliver valuable vitamins and minerals to support your body's various functions.

. . .

HEALTHY FATS ARE ALSO a key part of a nutrient-dense diet. They play a crucial role in providing long-lasting energy and supporting cellular function. Foods like avocados, nuts, seeds, and fatty fish are rich in monounsaturated and polyunsaturated fats, which are essential for overall health. Moreover, these foods are also rich in antioxidants, vitamins, and minerals that can support recovery and reduce inflammation.

WHEN CHOOSING CARBOHYDRATE-RICH FOODS, prioritize options that are high in fiber and nutrients, such as whole grains, fruits, and vegetables. Complex carbohydrates like brown rice, quinoa, and sweet potatoes provide sustained energy and help replenish glycogen stores, which are essential for muscle recovery.

IN ADDITION TO THE MACRONUTRIENTS, it's essential to pay attention to the micronutrients in your diet. These include vitamins and minerals like calcium, magnesium, and potassium, which play crucial roles in muscle function and recovery. Foods like dairy products, leafy greens, and bananas can provide these essential nutrients in a natural and bioavailable form.

HYDRATION IS another critical component of energy and recovery. Water plays a vital role in transporting nutrients, regulating body temperature, and promoting optimal cellular function. Be sure to drink plenty of water throughout the day, especially before, during, and after exercise to maintain proper hydration and support recovery.

WHEN PLANNING YOUR MEALS, consider the nutrient density of each food item and aim for a balance of protein, healthy fats, and complex carbohydrates. By doing so, you can ensure your body has the necessary building blocks to support energy production, muscle repair, and overall health.

. . .

Incorporating nutrient-dense foods into your daily diet doesn't have to be complicated or time-consuming. Simple strategies like adding a handful of spinach to your morning smoothie, snacking on a mix of nuts and seeds, or swapping out refined grains for whole grain options can make a significant difference in the quality of your diet.

By prioritizing nutrient-dense foods, you'll be well on your way to fueling your body with the energy and nutrients it needs to perform at its best. As you make these dietary changes, you'll likely notice improvements in your energy levels, recovery time, and overall well-being. Embrace the power of nutrient-dense foods and unlock the potential for a healthier, more vibrant life.

Hydration and Electrolyte Balance

Unlocking the secrets of hydration and electrolyte balance can transform your health, fitness, and overall well-being. When your body maintains optimal hydration and electrolyte levels, you can experience increased energy, improved athletic performance, and enhanced mental clarity. Let's dive into the importance of hydration and electrolyte balance and learn how to optimize these critical factors for better health.

Water is the foundation of life, playing a vital role in nearly every bodily function. It transports nutrients, flushes out toxins, regulates body temperature, and supports the proper functioning of cells, organs, and tissues. Despite its importance, many people struggle to maintain adequate hydration, leading to a variety of health issues ranging from fatigue to muscle cramps.

. . .

ELECTROLYTES ARE minerals that carry an electric charge and play a crucial role in maintaining the body's fluid balance, muscle function, and nerve signaling. Key electrolytes include sodium, potassium, calcium, magnesium, and chloride. These minerals can be found in various foods and beverages, and they're also lost through sweat, urine, and other bodily fluids.

STAYING hydrated and maintaining a proper electrolyte balance are particularly important for athletes and active individuals. During intense physical activity, the body loses significant amounts of water and electrolytes through sweat, leading to dehydration and an imbalance in electrolyte levels. This can result in reduced performance, muscle cramps, and even more serious health issues if left unchecked.

TO ENSURE you're properly hydrated, a general rule of thumb is to drink at least eight 8-ounce glasses of water per day. However, individual needs can vary based on factors such as body size, activity level, and climate. Pay attention to your body's signals, such as thirst, urine color, and overall energy levels, to determine if you're adequately hydrated.

WHEN IT COMES to electrolyte balance, consuming a balanced diet rich in whole foods can provide the necessary minerals to support proper function. Foods like bananas, avocados, spinach, and dairy products are excellent sources of essential electrolytes. In addition, sports drinks and electrolyte-enhanced water can be helpful for replenishing lost minerals during intense physical activity or hot weather.

ONE OFTEN OVERLOOKED aspect of hydration is the timing of fluid intake. Rather than chugging large amounts of water all at once, aim to sip fluids throughout the day, especially before, during, and after exercise. This can help maintain steady hydration levels and prevent sudden drops in electrolyte concentrations.

CAFFEINE AND ALCOHOL can have a diuretic effect, causing increased fluid loss through urine. While moderate consumption is generally safe, be mindful of the potential impact on your hydration status, and compensate by drinking additional water if needed.

REMEMBER that hydration and electrolyte balance are interconnected, and it's essential to address both factors to achieve optimal health. By prioritizing fluid intake and consuming a diet rich in electrolyte-containing foods, you can support your body's ability to perform at its best.

INCORPORATING these hydration and electrolyte balance strategies into your daily routine can lead to noticeable improvements in your energy levels, athletic performance, and overall well-being. By paying attention to your body's needs and making conscious choices, you can unlock the power of optimal hydration and electrolyte balance, setting the stage for a healthier, more vibrant life.

Customizing Your Nutrition Plan for Success

IMAGINE DESIGNING a nutrition plan that feels like it was created just for you, tailored to your unique needs, preferences, and goals. Customizing your nutrition plan can unlock new levels of success, helping you achieve your health, fitness, and wellness objectives. Let's explore the process of personalizing your nutrition plan and discover the keys to making it work for you.

. . .

ONE OF THE most important aspects of customizing your nutrition plan is understanding your body's specific needs. Factors such as age, weight, activity level, and health conditions all play a role in determining the right balance of nutrients for optimal health. Start by assessing your current needs and setting clear, achievable goals that align with your lifestyle.

A SUCCESSFUL NUTRITION plan hinges on the quality of the foods you choose. Focus on incorporating nutrient-dense whole foods, such as fruits, vegetables, lean proteins, and whole grains, into your daily meals. These foods provide the vitamins, minerals, and other essential nutrients your body needs to function at its best. By selecting foods that align with your preferences and dietary restrictions, you can create a plan that feels enjoyable and sustainable.

ANOTHER KEY ELEMENT of a customized nutrition plan is portion control. Understanding the appropriate serving sizes for different foods can help you balance your intake and prevent overeating. Use tools like measuring cups, food scales, or even your own hands as a guide to gauge portion sizes. This can empower you to make informed choices and maintain control over your consumption.

ACCOUNTING for your unique schedule and lifestyle is crucial when personalizing your nutrition plan. Consider factors like meal timing, meal frequency, and meal planning to create a plan that fits seamlessly into your daily routine. For example, if you prefer to eat several smaller meals throughout the day, structure your plan to include healthy snacks and smaller portions at each sitting.

CUSTOMIZING your nutrition plan also involves adapting it to support your fitness goals. If you're looking to build muscle or improve athletic performance, you may need to adjust your macronutrient ratios to include more protein or carbohydrates. Alternatively, if your goal is weight loss, you may need to create a calorie deficit by reducing your overall intake or increasing physical activity.

As you build your personalized nutrition plan, it's essential to remain flexible and open to change. Regularly evaluate your progress and adjust your plan as needed to ensure it continues to serve your evolving needs and goals. This may involve tweaking portion sizes, experimenting with new foods, or making other modifications to better align with your objectives.

Support is a vital component of any successful nutrition plan. Share your goals with friends, family, or a professional nutritionist to create a network of accountability and encouragement. This can help you stay on track and motivated as you work towards achieving your desired outcomes.

Crafting a customized nutrition plan is a dynamic and ongoing process, but the rewards are well worth the effort. By understanding your body's unique needs, focusing on whole foods, and adapting your plan to support your goals, you can create a sustainable and enjoyable approach to nutrition. Embrace the journey of personalization, and watch as your health, fitness, and overall well-being flourish.

7

BOOSTING ATHLETIC PERFORMANCE
ELEVATING YOUR FITNESS WITH THE WIM HOF METHOD

Enhancing Endurance and Strength through Breathing Techniques

Unlocking the power of breath is a game-changer for enhancing endurance and strength in both fitness and everyday life. With proper breathing techniques, you can tap into a wellspring of energy, focus, and resilience. Let's delve into how you can harness the power of your breath to optimize your performance and reach new heights in your physical pursuits.

AN ESSENTIAL COMPONENT of effective breathing is mastering diaphragmatic breathing, or belly breathing. This technique involves using your diaphragm, the primary muscle responsible for respiration, to draw air deep into your lungs. By engaging your diaphragm, you can increase oxygen intake and improve overall lung capacity. Practice diaphragmatic breathing by placing one hand on your chest and the other on your abdomen, taking slow, deep breaths, and feeling your belly rise and fall as you breathe.

ONCE YOU'VE HONED your diaphragmatic breathing skills, you can begin to integrate specific techniques tailored to your chosen activities. For example, endurance athletes like runners or cyclists can benefit from rhythmic breathing, which involves synchronizing your breath with your movements. This method not only helps maintain a steady flow of oxygen to working muscles but also encourages proper form and reduces the risk of injury.

STRENGTH TRAINING, on the other hand, can benefit from the Valsalva maneuver, a technique that involves holding your breath and tightening your core muscles during the most challenging part of a lift. This creates intra-abdominal pressure, stabilizes your spine, and allows you to generate more force. Remember to exhale forcefully once you've completed the lift to avoid lightheadedness or dizziness.

ANOTHER POWERFUL BREATHING technique to consider is box breathing, also known as four-square breathing. This method is particularly useful for managing stress and promoting relaxation, both of which are critical for optimal athletic performance. To practice box breathing, find a comfortable position and inhale deeply through your nose for a count of four, hold your breath for another count of four, exhale through your mouth for four counts, and then hold your breath again for a final count of four. Repeat this cycle several times to help calm your mind and prepare your body for the task ahead.

MINDFULNESS PLAYS a significant role in effective breathing as well. Developing a greater awareness of your breath and its connection to your body can help you maintain control during physical activity. Whether you're engaging in high-intensity interval training, practicing yoga, or simply going for a walk, mindfulness can enhance the benefits of your chosen breathing techniques and improve your overall performance.

AS WITH ANY NEW SKILL, practice is key when it comes to mastering breathing techniques. Dedicate time each day to focus on your breath, whether during exercise, meditation, or simply when going about your daily activities. By building your breathing practice into your daily routine, you can create lasting habits that support your endurance, strength, and overall well-being.

INCORPORATING effective breathing techniques into your fitness and wellness routine can unlock untapped potential and elevate your performance to new heights. By mastering diaphragmatic breathing and exploring techniques tailored to your specific activities, you can enhance your endurance, increase your strength, and better manage stress. Embrace the power of breath and discover the transformative impact it can have on your physical pursuits and overall well-being.

Optimizing Recovery with Cold Exposure

IMAGINE SUPERCHARGING your recovery process and boosting your overall well-being with the power of cold exposure. This might sound intense, but the benefits of incorporating cold therapy into your routine are truly remarkable. Let's dive into the world of cold exposure and learn how to optimize recovery, improve athletic performance, and enhance mental resilience.

COLD EXPOSURE, also known as cryotherapy or cold therapy, involves exposing your body to cold temperatures for short periods of time. The most common methods include cold showers, ice baths, and cryotherapy chambers. These chilly treatments have been shown to help reduce inflammation, accelerate muscle recovery, and even improve mood.

WHEN IT COMES to reducing inflammation, cold exposure works its magic by constricting blood vessels and limiting blood flow to the affected area. This natural response can help alleviate pain and swelling in overworked muscles. For athletes and fitness enthusiasts alike, incorporating cold exposure into a recovery routine can be a game-changer.

A POPULAR AND accessible method of cold exposure is the cold shower. While it might sound daunting at first, incorporating a brief cold shower into your daily routine can yield impressive results. Begin with lukewarm water, and gradually decrease the temperature as you acclimate to the sensation. Aim for a duration of two to three minutes initially, and gradually increase the time as you become more comfortable with the experience.

If you're looking to take cold exposure to the next level, consider trying an ice bath. Submerging your body in a tub filled with ice and cold water for 10 to 15 minutes can help accelerate muscle recovery and reduce soreness. Just remember to ease into the practice, starting with shorter durations and gradually increasing the time as your body adapts.

For those seeking a more controlled environment, cryotherapy chambers offer a cutting-edge approach to cold exposure. During a cryotherapy session, you'll enter a chamber filled with cold air, with temperatures reaching as low as -200°F. The treatment typically lasts between two and three minutes and can provide similar benefits to ice baths, such as reduced inflammation and improved recovery.

Aside from its physical benefits, cold exposure can also have a positive impact on mental health. Regular cold therapy has been linked to the release of mood-boosting endorphins, leading to increased feelings of well-being and reduced symptoms of anxiety and depression. Furthermore, the act of voluntarily exposing yourself to discomfort can help build mental resilience, enhancing your ability to cope with stress and overcome challenges.

Before starting cold exposure, it's crucial to listen to your body and approach the practice with caution. Consult with a healthcare professional if you have any concerns or underlying health conditions. Remember, the key to success with cold exposure is consistency and gradual progression, so take it slow and steady.

. . .

INTEGRATING cold exposure into your recovery routine can have a profound impact on your physical and mental well-being. By experimenting with methods such as cold showers, ice baths, or cryotherapy, you can unlock the power of cold to reduce inflammation, speed up muscle recovery, and enhance mental resilience. Embrace the chill, and discover the transformative potential of cold exposure as a tool for optimizing recovery and reaching new heights in your athletic pursuits and everyday life.

Incorporating Mindfulness for Mental Toughness

EXPERIENCE the power of mindfulness to forge mental toughness, paving the way for personal growth, resilience, and a deepened sense of self-awareness. The journey begins here, as we delve into the world of mindfulness, explore its practical applications, and learn how to harness its potential to transform our lives.

MINDFULNESS, the art of paying attention to the present moment with curiosity and nonjudgment, invites us to cultivate a deeper understanding of our thoughts, emotions, and physical sensations. By honing our awareness, we develop the ability to respond skillfully to life's challenges, even in the face of adversity.

MEDITATION, a cornerstone of mindfulness, provides a gateway to inner peace and mental clarity. Sitting in stillness, focusing on the breath, and observing the ebb and flow of thoughts, we learn to be present with ourselves and gently redirect our attention when our minds wander. This consistent practice nurtures emotional regulation and bolsters resilience, fortifying our mental toughness.

OF COURSE, meditation is just one path toward mindfulness. Everyday activities present countless opportunities to practice.

Engage fully in ordinary tasks such as washing dishes, walking, or eating, and immerse yourself in the experience. Attending to the task at hand, observe your thoughts and sensations as they arise, and welcome each moment with open arms.

WHEN CHALLENGES ARISE, mindfulness becomes a steadfast companion. Recognizing the signs of stress and anxiety, we can pause, breathe, and take note of our thoughts and bodily sensations. This simple yet powerful act of awareness paves the way for thoughtful, deliberate decision-making, even in the face of adversity.

MINDFULNESS AND A GROWTH MINDSET, the belief that intelligence and abilities can be developed through dedication and hard work, go hand in hand. Embrace this mindset, and you'll be more likely to persevere when faced with challenges, viewing them as opportunities for learning and growth. As you practice mindfulness, acknowledge any self-limiting beliefs that emerge, and gently challenge them with curiosity and compassion.

SELF-COMPASSION, too, plays a pivotal role in mental toughness. Mindfulness teaches us to extend kindness and understanding toward ourselves, even when we falter or encounter setbacks. Instead of harsh self-criticism, adopt a compassionate inner dialogue, acknowledging your struggles and offering support and encouragement, as you would for a dear friend.

MAINTAINING a connection to our values and a sense of purpose is vital for mental toughness. Regularly reflect on your goals and aspirations, ensuring that your actions align with your core beliefs and contribute to the life you desire. This intentional living empowers us to persevere through challenges and setbacks, as we stay true to our authentic selves.

. . .

So take a moment to pause, breathe, and connect with the present moment, for the journey toward mental toughness and personal growth has already begun, right here and right now.

Setting and Achieving Your Fitness Goals

Unlock your fitness potential by setting and achieving your goals, transforming your body, and nurturing your mind. Delve into the realm of fitness goal-setting and discover practical strategies to overcome obstacles and fuel your motivation for success.

Begin by establishing clear, specific, and realistic fitness goals. Instead of vague aspirations such as "getting in shape" or "losing weight," pinpoint precise targets like running a 5K, improving flexibility, or shedding a certain number of pounds. By defining your objectives, you create a roadmap for your fitness journey, enabling you to measure your progress and celebrate your accomplishments.

Remember to set both short-term and long-term goals, as this approach encourages sustained motivation and a sense of achievement. Short-term goals offer milestones to celebrate and motivate, while long-term objectives provide direction and a sense of purpose. As you reach each short-term goal, reassess your long-term vision and adjust your plan accordingly to keep moving forward.

Accountability is paramount in the pursuit of fitness goals. Enlist the support of friends, family, or workout partners who can offer encouragement, guidance, and a gentle nudge when needed. Alternatively, consider joining a workout group or engaging a personal trainer to provide structure, guidance, and support tailored to your specific goals.

STAY MOTIVATED by incorporating variety into your fitness routine. Experiment with different types of workouts and activities, from strength training to yoga to swimming. This approach not only keeps boredom at bay but also ensures that you challenge your body in diverse ways, promoting well-rounded fitness and reducing the risk of plateaus or injury.

TRACKING your progress is essential for maintaining momentum and evaluating the effectiveness of your fitness plan. Use a journal, spreadsheet, or fitness app to document your workouts, physical changes, and personal bests. Regularly reviewing this data provides insight into your progress and highlights areas for improvement, empowering you to make informed decisions about your training.

WHEN SETBACKS OR OBSTACLES ARISE, as they inevitably will, draw upon your resilience and determination to push through. Reframe challenges as opportunities for growth and learning, and remind yourself of your reasons for pursuing your fitness goals. When necessary, adjust your plan or timeline to accommodate unexpected hurdles, but never lose sight of your ultimate objectives.

CELEBRATE YOUR ACCOMPLISHMENTS, both large and small, as these victories fuel your motivation and boost your self-esteem. Reward yourself for achieving milestones with non-food treats, such as a massage, a new workout outfit, or a special experience. By reinforcing your achievements with positive reinforcement, you strengthen your commitment to your fitness journey and foster a sense of accomplishment.

. . .

MAINTAINING a balanced perspective is crucial for sustainable fitness success. Avoid becoming consumed by your goals or neglecting other aspects of your life, such as relationships or self-care. Strive for a holistic approach to well-being that encompasses physical, mental, and emotional health.

EMBRACE the power of setting and achieving fitness goals as a catalyst for personal transformation. By establishing specific objectives, seeking support, staying motivated, tracking progress, overcoming obstacles, and celebrating victories, you set the stage for a healthier, happier, and more fulfilled life. Your fitness journey begins with a single step, so lace up your sneakers and embark on the path to success.

8

CULTIVATING RESILIENCE
OVERCOMING STRESS AND ANXIETY WITH THE WIM HOF METHOD

The Science of Stress and Its Impact on Your Body

Stress is an omnipresent force in modern life, and understanding the science behind it can empower you to mitigate its impact on your body and well-being. Grasp the intricacies of stress, its physiological effects, and the strategies to manage it effectively for a healthier and more balanced life.

AT ITS CORE, stress is a biological response to perceived threats or challenges, activating the body's "fight or flight" mechanism. This response releases a cascade of hormones, including adrenaline and cortisol, that prompt various physical changes, such as increased heart rate, rapid breathing, and heightened alertness. While this reaction can be beneficial in short bursts – for instance, during a sports competition or an emergency – chronic stress can have detrimental effects on overall health.

ONE AREA where stress takes a considerable toll is the immune system. Studies have shown that chronic stress can weaken immune function, making the body more susceptible to infections and illnesses. Furthermore, it can prolong the healing process, complicating recovery from injuries or surgical procedures.

THE CARDIOVASCULAR SYSTEM is another target of stress. Persistent stress can lead to elevated blood pressure, increased heart rate, and the constriction of blood vessels, all of which increase the risk of developing heart disease or suffering a stroke. Researchers have also linked stress to the buildup of plaque in the arteries, which can obstruct blood flow and precipitate heart attacks.

MENTAL HEALTH IS NOT immune to the effects of stress either. Exposure to chronic stress can trigger or exacerbate anxiety and depression, as well as contribute to the development of other mental health disorders. Moreover, stress can impair cognitive functions, such as memory and concentration, hindering academic and professional performance.

DESPITE THE SEEMINGLY OVERWHELMING influence of stress, there are ways to counteract its impact on your body and well-being. One effective strategy is to engage in regular physical activity. Exercise stimulates the production of endorphins – the body's "feel-good" hormones – which can help alleviate stress and bolster mood. Aim for at least 30 minutes of moderate-intensity exercise most days of the week to reap the stress-busting benefits.

ANOTHER TECHNIQUE TO combat stress is through mindfulness and meditation. Practicing mindfulness involves focusing on the present moment, observing thoughts and feelings without judgment. Meditation, a more structured form of mindfulness, has been shown to reduce stress and promote relaxation by activating the body's relaxation response – the counterbalance to the stress response. Incorporate daily mindfulness or meditation sessions into your routine to foster a sense of calm and clarity.

QUALITY SLEEP IS ALSO crucial for managing stress and maintaining overall health. Strive for seven to nine hours of uninterrupted sleep each night, establishing a consistent bedtime routine and creating a sleep-conducive environment. Sleep allows the body to recover and rejuvenate, helping to mitigate the impact of stress on your well-being.

FINALLY, nurturing social connections can serve as a potent buffer against stress. Establishing and maintaining strong relationships with friends and family members provides emotional support, a sense of belonging, and a sounding board for discussing problems and concerns. Make an effort to connect with loved ones regularly, whether through phone calls, video chats, or in-person gatherings.

BY UNDERSTANDING the science of stress and its impact on the body, you can take proactive steps to manage its influence and safeguard your health. Through regular exercise, mindfulness, quality sleep, and social connections, you can cultivate resilience in the face of life's inevitable challenges and pave the way for a more balanced and fulfilling life.

Strategies for Managing Stress through Breathing and Cold Exposure

HARNESS THE POWER of your breath and embrace the chill of cold exposure to manage stress and enhance well-being. These simple yet potent techniques offer a natural, accessible way to mitigate stress and promote a sense of balance in your life.

BREATHING EXERCISES, long recognized for their calming effects, provide an immediate and effective means of stress relief. One such technique is diaphragmatic breathing, also known as deep or belly breathing. This involves inhaling deeply through the nose, allowing the diaphragm to expand and the stomach to rise, followed by a slow exhale through the mouth. The process stimulates the vagus nerve, which in turn activates the parasympathetic nervous system – responsible for the body's relaxation response. Incorporate diaphragmatic breathing into your daily routine, practicing for a few minutes each day to foster relaxation and reduce stress levels.

ANOTHER POWERFUL BREATHING method is the 4-7-8 technique, which involves inhaling through the nose for a count of four, holding the breath for a count of seven, and exhaling through the mouth for a count of eight. This exercise promotes relaxation by slowing the heart rate and calming the mind. Commit to practicing the 4-7-8 technique twice daily for optimal stress management benefits.

BEYOND BREATHWORK, cold exposure has emerged as an innovative way to manage stress and improve overall well-being. Cold showers, ice baths, and cold plunges are popular methods of introducing the body to lower temperatures. While the thought of embracing the cold may seem daunting, research suggests that cold exposure can offer numerous health benefits, including reduced stress levels, increased alertness, and enhanced mood.

COLD EXPOSURE WORKS by activating the body's adaptive stress response, which helps build resilience and promotes the release of mood-boosting chemicals, such as endorphins and norepinephrine. Additionally, cold exposure can increase the body's production of brown adipose tissue – a type of fat that generates heat and helps regulate body temperature.

IF YOU'RE new to cold exposure, start by introducing short, cold showers into your daily routine. Begin with a warm shower and gradually reduce the water temperature, aiming to immerse yourself in the cold water for at least 30 seconds. Over time, increase the duration of cold exposure to reap the full stress-relieving benefits.

FOR THOSE SEEKING A MORE intense cold experience, consider trying ice baths or cold plunges. Submerge your body in ice-cold water for a few minutes, focusing on your breath to maintain calm and relaxation. Though challenging, this practice can offer a powerful boost to both mental and physical well-being.

. . .

When incorporating breathing exercises and cold exposure into your stress management toolkit, it's essential to listen to your body and adjust the techniques to suit your individual needs. Always practice these methods in a safe environment and consult with a healthcare professional if you have any concerns or pre-existing medical conditions.

As you embrace the power of your breath and the invigorating chill of cold exposure, you'll find yourself better equipped to manage stress and cultivate resilience in the face of life's inevitable challenges. Integrating these techniques into your daily routine can lead to a more balanced, vibrant, and fulfilling life, offering you the tools to navigate the complexities of modern living with grace and ease.

Building Mental Resilience with Mindfulness Practices

Cultivate mental resilience and inner strength through mindfulness practices, transforming how you face challenges and experience life. By integrating these simple yet powerful techniques into your daily routine, you can foster a more balanced and grounded mindset, allowing you to navigate life's hurdles with greater ease and confidence.

Mindfulness, at its core, involves cultivating a non-judgmental awareness of the present moment. One of the most accessible and widely practiced mindfulness techniques is meditation. By setting aside a few minutes each day to meditate, you can develop a greater sense of clarity, focus, and emotional stability. To begin, find a quiet and comfortable space, sit upright, and gently close your eyes. Focus your attention on your breath, noticing the sensation of each inhale and exhale. When your mind wanders, gently bring your focus back to your breath, without judgment or criticism. Over time, this practice can lead to improved concentration, reduced stress, and increased resilience in the face of life's challenges.

ANOTHER MINDFULNESS PRACTICE that can bolster mental resilience is the body scan meditation. This technique involves systematically directing your attention to different parts of the body, observing any sensations or tension without judgment. Starting at the top of your head and moving down to your toes, the body scan can help you develop a greater awareness of your physical presence and release any accumulated stress. Regular practice of body scan meditation can enhance your ability to cope with physical discomfort and foster a deeper mind-body connection.

PRACTICING gratitude is another powerful way to cultivate mental resilience through mindfulness. By intentionally focusing on the positive aspects of your life, you can shift your perspective and foster a greater sense of well-being. To incorporate gratitude into your daily routine, consider keeping a gratitude journal, where you list three things you're grateful for each day. Over time, this practice can help you develop a more optimistic outlook and better navigate difficult situations.

MINDFULNESS PRACTICES CAN ALSO BE INTEGRATED into everyday activities, such as walking, eating, or even engaging in conversation. For example, during a mindful walk, focus your attention on the sensation of your feet touching the ground, the rhythm of your breath, and the surrounding environment. Similarly, when eating, slow down and savor each bite, noticing the flavors, textures, and aromas of your food. Engaging in these everyday mindfulness practices can enhance your overall sense of presence and awareness.

. . .

IN ADDITION to these individual practices, consider exploring group mindfulness activities or workshops, which can offer a supportive environment for deepening your practice and connecting with others. Participating in a mindfulness-based stress reduction (MBSR) program or attending a meditation retreat can provide valuable guidance and opportunities for growth.

AS YOU EMBRACE mindfulness practices and weave them into the fabric of your daily life, you'll begin to notice a profound shift in your mental resilience and overall well-being. Faced with life's inevitable ups and downs, you'll be better equipped to respond with grace, clarity, and inner strength. By nurturing your mind and cultivating a present-moment awareness, you can foster a more balanced and fulfilling life, allowing you to thrive even in the face of adversity.

Developing Healthy Habits for Long-Term Stress Management

EMBRACE the power of healthy habits to foster long-term stress management, enhancing your well-being and allowing you to thrive in every aspect of life. By incorporating these habits into your daily routine, you can lay the foundation for a more balanced and resilient lifestyle, ultimately boosting your ability to cope with life's challenges.

ONE CORNERSTONE of stress management is regular physical activity. Exercise not only improves physical health but also plays a vital role in reducing stress and enhancing mental well-being. By engaging in activities you enjoy, whether it's jogging, dancing, or swimming, you can increase the production of feel-good endorphins, boosting your mood and providing a natural form of stress relief. Aim to engage in moderate-intensity exercise for at least 150 minutes per week to reap the full benefits.

. . .

A WELL-BALANCED DIET is another essential component of long-term stress management. By nourishing your body with nutrient-dense foods, you can support optimal brain function and mental health. Focus on incorporating whole foods such as fruits, vegetables, lean proteins, and whole grains into your meals, while minimizing processed foods and added sugars. Additionally, staying hydrated by drinking plenty of water throughout the day can help regulate mood and reduce the impact of stress on your body.

PRIORITIZING quality sleep is crucial for managing stress and maintaining overall well-being. Adequate rest allows your body to recover from daily stressors and enhances cognitive function. To improve your sleep hygiene, establish a consistent sleep schedule, create a relaxing bedtime routine, and optimize your sleep environment by reducing light and noise. Aim for 7-9 hours of sleep per night to ensure you wake up refreshed and ready to tackle the day ahead.

DEVELOPING a strong support system can also play a significant role in stress management. By building and maintaining connections with friends, family, and colleagues, you can share your experiences, gain new perspectives, and foster a sense of belonging. Make time for social activities and engage in meaningful conversations to strengthen your support network, which can serve as a valuable resource when navigating challenging situations.

INCORPORATING relaxation techniques into your daily routine can further enhance your ability to manage stress. Practices such as deep breathing exercises, progressive muscle relaxation, and visualization can help you calm your mind and release tension from your body. By setting aside time each day to practice these techniques, you can cultivate a greater sense of inner peace and resilience.

FINALLY, consider seeking professional help if you find yourself struggling to manage stress on your own. A mental health professional can provide valuable guidance and support, helping you develop personalized strategies for coping with stress and improving your overall well-being.

BY INTEGRATING these healthy habits into your daily life, you can create a solid foundation for long-term stress management, enhancing your well-being and empowering you to thrive in the face of life's challenges. Remember, cultivating a resilient and balanced lifestyle is an ongoing process, and it's essential to remain patient and compassionate with yourself as you navigate this journey. With dedication, consistency, and self-care, you can build the skills necessary to effectively manage stress and create a more fulfilling and vibrant life.

9

THE WIM HOF METHOD FOR ALL AGES

ADAPTING THE PRACTICE FOR DIFFERENT LIFE STAGES

The Wim Hof Method for Children and Adolescents

Unlock the potential of the Wim Hof Method for children and adolescents, empowering them to cultivate resilience, boost their immune system, and develop a strong foundation for lifelong well-being. By introducing young people to this transformative practice, you can help them navigate the challenges of life with greater ease, confidence, and a sense of inner balance.

THE WIM HOF METHOD, developed by Dutch extreme athlete Wim Hof, comprises three primary components: cold exposure, controlled breathing, and mindset training. Combined, these elements work synergistically to improve mental and physical health, making it an ideal practice for children and adolescents who face a myriad of stressors in today's fast-paced world.

COLD EXPOSURE, such as cold showers or ice baths, might seem intimidating at first, but they offer numerous benefits for young people. These benefits include increased resilience, improved circulation, and a strengthened immune response. When introducing cold exposure to children, it's crucial to start slowly and incrementally. Encourage them to begin with lukewarm showers, gradually decreasing the temperature over time to ensure their safety and comfort.

CONTROLLED breathing exercises are another essential component of the Wim Hof Method. By teaching children and adolescents to breathe mindfully and intentionally, you can help them develop greater self-awareness, emotional regulation, and stress management skills. One simple yet effective exercise involves slow, deep breaths through the nose, followed by a gentle exhale through the mouth. Encourage young people to practice this technique for a few minutes each day, gradually increasing the duration as they become more comfortable and proficient.

MINDSET TRAINING IS the third pillar of the Wim Hof Method, which focuses on fostering a positive outlook and strong mental resilience. By teaching children and adolescents to set goals, visualize success, and maintain a growth mindset, you can equip them with the tools necessary to overcome challenges and reach their full potential. Encourage young people to practice affirmations, positive self-talk, and gratitude exercises to cultivate an optimistic and resilient mindset.

IT'S important to recognize that every child and adolescent is unique, and their experience with the Wim Hof Method will differ accordingly. When introducing this practice to young people, be mindful of their individual needs, limitations, and preferences. Offer guidance, support, and encouragement, while emphasizing the importance of listening to their bodies and honoring their personal boundaries.

AS WITH ANY NEW PRACTICE, consistency is key. Encourage children and adolescents to incorporate the Wim Hof Method into their daily routines, reminding them that progress takes time and patience. By celebrating small victories and acknowledging their efforts, you can foster a sense of accomplishment and motivation that will propel them forward in their journey.

IN ADDITION to the physical and mental health benefits, the Wim Hof Method can provide valuable opportunities for family bonding and connection. By practicing the method together, parents and children can support one another, share experiences, and create lasting memories. This shared experience can strengthen family relationships and create a foundation of trust, understanding, and mutual growth.

. . .

THE WIM HOF METHOD has the potential to transform the lives of children and adolescents, equipping them with the skills, resilience, and inner strength necessary to navigate the complexities of modern life. By introducing this powerful practice to young people, you can empower them to cultivate a strong foundation for lifelong well-being, enabling them to thrive in the face of life's challenges and unlock their full potential.

Tailoring the Practice for Adults and Seniors

EMBRACE the art of tailoring wellness practices for adults and seniors, allowing individuals to reap the benefits of a healthy lifestyle at every stage of life. By customizing these practices, you can help older adults enhance their physical and mental well-being, maintain their independence, and foster a sense of purpose and fulfillment.

AS WE AGE, our bodies and minds undergo various changes, making it essential to adapt wellness practices to suit the unique needs and limitations of older individuals. For adults and seniors, a focus on low-impact activities that promote flexibility, balance, and strength is crucial. Examples of such activities include yoga, tai chi, and swimming, which are gentle on the joints while providing numerous health benefits.

IN ADDITION TO PHYSICAL ACTIVITY, mindfulness practices play a vital role in maintaining mental well-being as we age. Encourage older adults to engage in meditation, deep breathing exercises, and other forms of relaxation techniques. These practices can help reduce stress, improve focus, and enhance emotional resilience, all of which contribute to a healthier and more fulfilling life.

NUTRITION IS another key factor in tailoring wellness practices for adults and seniors. As our dietary needs evolve with age, it's essential to adopt a balanced and nutrient-rich diet that supports optimal health. Encourage older individuals to consume whole foods, such as fruits, vegetables, whole grains, lean proteins, and healthy fats, while minimizing processed foods and added sugars. Additionally, staying hydrated is crucial for maintaining cognitive function and overall health.

IT'S important to recognize that social connections play a significant role in the well-being of older adults. Foster opportunities for social engagement, such as group classes, community events, and intergenerational activities. By nurturing meaningful relationships, adults and seniors can combat feelings of isolation and loneliness, while enjoying a sense of belonging and support.

WHEN IT COMES to tailoring wellness practices for adults and seniors, it's essential to consider the individual's unique circumstances, interests, and limitations. Be sure to consult with healthcare professionals, such as doctors or physical therapists, to ensure the chosen activities are safe and appropriate for the individual. Moreover, encourage older adults to listen to their bodies and modify exercises as needed to prevent injury and maximize the benefits.

CONSISTENCY AND ROUTINE are vital components of any wellness practice. Help adults and seniors create a sustainable plan that incorporates physical activity, mindfulness, nutrition, and social engagement. By establishing a regular routine, older individuals can more easily integrate these practices into their daily lives, ultimately promoting long-term health and well-being.

. . .

Lastly, keep in mind that motivation and a sense of purpose can significantly impact the success of any wellness practice. Encourage older adults to set realistic and meaningful goals, celebrate their achievements, and focus on the positive aspects of their progress. By cultivating a growth mindset and a sense of self-efficacy, adults and seniors can maintain their motivation and enthusiasm for their wellness journey.

In conclusion, tailoring wellness practices for adults and seniors is an essential step in promoting lifelong well-being and fulfillment. By considering the unique needs, interests, and limitations of older individuals, you can help them create a personalized and sustainable plan that supports their physical and mental health. Through a combination of low-impact activities, mindfulness practices, balanced nutrition, and social engagement, adults and seniors can enjoy a vibrant and meaningful life, regardless of their age.

Modifying the Method for Pregnant Women and Postpartum Recovery

Pregnancy and the postpartum period present unique challenges and opportunities for wellness. For pregnant women, the focus should be on gentle exercises that promote strength, flexibility, and relaxation. Prenatal yoga, for example, is an excellent choice, as it can help ease common pregnancy discomforts, prepare the body for labor, and encourage a deeper connection with the growing baby.

In addition to physical activity, mindfulness practices can significantly impact the well-being of pregnant women. Encourage expectant mothers to engage in meditation, deep breathing exercises, and other relaxation techniques to alleviate stress, improve focus, and foster a sense of calm during pregnancy.

NUTRITION IS another essential aspect of wellness for pregnant women. Emphasize the importance of a balanced diet that provides essential nutrients for both mother and baby. Encourage the consumption of whole foods, such as fruits, vegetables, whole grains, lean proteins, and healthy fats, while minimizing processed foods and added sugars. Additionally, staying hydrated is crucial for maintaining energy levels and supporting a healthy pregnancy.

WHEN IT COMES to postpartum recovery, a gradual reintroduction of physical activity is essential. New moms should consult with healthcare professionals before resuming exercise, and consider activities that gently support the body's healing process. Postnatal yoga and low-impact exercises, such as walking or swimming, can help restore strength, flexibility, and overall well-being.

POSTPARTUM MINDFULNESS PRACTICES can also play a significant role in supporting new mothers' emotional health. Encourage the practice of meditation, deep breathing, and other relaxation techniques to help reduce stress, improve mood, and promote a sense of balance during this time of transition.

BREASTFEEDING mothers should pay special attention to their nutrition, as it directly impacts both their well-being and their baby's growth. Emphasize the importance of a nutrient-rich diet, focusing on whole foods, lean proteins, and healthy fats, while staying hydrated to support optimal milk production.

IT'S important to recognize that social connections and support are vital during pregnancy and postpartum recovery. Encourage pregnant women and new mothers to seek out community resources, such as prenatal classes, support groups, and new mom meet-ups. By building a network of support, women can share experiences, learn from one another, and foster a sense of belonging during this life-changing period.

When modifying wellness practices for pregnant women and postpartum recovery, it's essential to consider the individual's unique circumstances, interests, and limitations. Always consult with healthcare professionals to ensure that chosen activities are safe and appropriate. Moreover, encourage women to listen to their bodies and adjust their practices as needed to support their changing needs.

Consistency and routine play crucial roles in establishing and maintaining wellness practices during pregnancy and postpartum recovery. Help expectant and new moms create a sustainable plan that incorporates physical activity, mindfulness, nutrition, and social support. By establishing a regular routine, they can more easily integrate these practices into their daily lives, ultimately promoting long-term health and well-being.

Adapting the Wim Hof Method for Individuals with Health Conditions and Disabilities

One crucial aspect of adapting the Wim Hof Method is tailoring the breathing exercises to suit each individual's capacity. For those with respiratory issues, such as asthma or COPD, it's essential to consult a healthcare professional before engaging in deep-breathing exercises. These individuals may benefit from milder forms of breathwork that emphasize slow, controlled inhalations and exhalations, promoting relaxation without causing undue strain on the respiratory system.

. . .

SIMILARLY, individuals with heart conditions or high blood pressure should approach the Wim Hof Method with caution. While the method has been shown to improve cardiovascular health for some, it may not be appropriate for everyone. Consulting a healthcare professional and opting for gentler, more controlled breathing exercises can help mitigate risks while still offering the benefits of relaxation and stress reduction.

THE COLD EXPOSURE component of the Wim Hof Method can also be modified to accommodate individual needs. While cold showers or ice baths may be too intense for some, there are alternative ways to experience the benefits of cold exposure. For example, individuals can start by simply splashing cold water on their face or using a cold compress on the back of their neck. Gradually increasing the duration and intensity of cold exposure can help individuals build resilience and adapt to the practice in a safe, controlled manner.

FOR INDIVIDUALS WITH PHYSICAL DISABILITIES, the Wim Hof Method's emphasis on movement and stretching may require adaptation. Working with a physical therapist or personal trainer can be invaluable in creating a customized program that takes into account specific limitations and abilities. Yoga, tai chi, or other low-impact exercises can be excellent alternatives that promote flexibility, strength, and balance.

WHEN ADAPTING the Wim Hof Method for individuals with health conditions and disabilities, it's essential to consider the role of mindfulness and mental resilience. Practicing meditation, visualization, or other mindfulness techniques can help individuals connect with their inner strength and develop the mental fortitude to overcome challenges. Encourage the exploration of different mindfulness practices to find the approach that resonates most with each person.

It's important to recognize that the process of adapting the Wim Hof Method will be unique for every individual, depending on their specific needs and abilities. Encourage open communication and collaboration with healthcare professionals, therapists, and trainers to develop a safe and effective plan tailored to each person's circumstances.

Finally, remember that consistency and commitment are key to experiencing the full benefits of the Wim Hof Method, regardless of one's abilities or health conditions. Encourage individuals to establish a regular routine and continually reassess and adjust their practices as needed. By fostering a growth mindset and embracing the idea of continuous improvement, individuals can unlock their potential for transformation and well-being.

In essence, adapting the Wim Hof Method for individuals with health conditions and disabilities can open the door to improved physical, mental, and emotional well-being. By considering each person's unique needs and limitations, and collaborating with healthcare professionals and support networks, it's possible to create a tailored plan that empowers individuals to overcome challenges and embrace a healthier, more resilient life.

10

THE WIM HOF LIFESTYLE
EMBRACING A HOLISTIC APPROACH TO HEALTH AND WELL-BEING

Expanding Your Horizons: Exploring Other Complementary Practices

Expand your horizons and enrich your personal growth journey by exploring complementary practices that enhance your overall well-being. By incorporating diverse approaches, you can unlock new dimensions of self-discovery and transformation, creating a harmonious balance of mind, body, and spirit.

MEDITATION IS an excellent complementary practice that cultivates mindfulness, reduces stress, and fosters inner peace. Various meditation techniques, such as focused attention, open monitoring, or loving-kindness meditation, cater to different preferences and goals. Experiment with these techniques to find the one that resonates most with you, and establish a regular practice to experience the full benefits of meditation.

YOGA IS another practice that beautifully complements a holistic approach to well-being. Combining physical postures, breathing exercises, and meditation, yoga promotes flexibility, strength, and relaxation. With numerous styles to choose from, such as Hatha, Vinyasa, or Yin Yoga, there's a practice for everyone, regardless of experience or fitness level. Seek out beginner-friendly classes or online resources to embark on your yoga journey.

NUTRITION PLAYS a crucial role in supporting overall health and well-being, making it an essential complementary practice to explore. Focus on incorporating whole, nutrient-dense foods into your diet, while minimizing processed, high-sugar options. To ensure a balanced approach, consider consulting with a nutritionist or registered dietitian who can provide personalized guidance based on your specific needs and goals.

THE POWER of community and social connection cannot be underestimated when exploring complementary practices. Engaging with like-minded individuals through support groups, workshops, or classes can provide valuable encouragement, motivation, and camaraderie. Sharing experiences, challenges, and successes with others can be a transformative experience that propels personal growth.

INCORPORATING elements of nature into your well-being journey can also be highly beneficial. Activities such as hiking, forest bathing, or simply spending time outdoors can help reduce stress, boost mood, and promote a sense of connectedness with the natural world. By embracing the healing power of nature, you can foster a deeper appreciation for your surroundings and cultivate a sense of harmony within yourself.

EXPRESSIVE ARTS, such as painting, writing, or dancing, can be a powerful tool for self-exploration and emotional release. These creative practices encourage self-expression and foster emotional resilience, making them a valuable addition to any personal growth journey. Seek out workshops, classes, or online resources to explore different forms of expressive arts, and embrace the process without judgment or expectation.

LASTLY, don't be afraid to explore alternative healing modalities, such as acupuncture, Reiki, or sound therapy. These practices often have roots in ancient wisdom and have been used for centuries to promote balance, healing, and well-being. Approach these modalities with an open mind and a willingness to explore, and you may discover new avenues for growth and healing.

ULTIMATELY, the key to expanding your horizons and exploring complementary practices is to approach each opportunity with curiosity, openness, and a willingness to learn. As you engage with diverse practices and disciplines, remain patient and allow yourself the time and space to grow. Embrace the journey, recognizing that each experience offers valuable insights and lessons that contribute to your overall well-being and personal growth. By combining these complementary practices, you can create a holistic, multi-faceted approach to self-discovery and transformation that supports a balanced, fulfilled life.

Staying Inspired: Following Wim Hof and Other Influencers

STAYING INSPIRED IS a powerful motivator in any self-improvement journey, and following the teachings of Wim Hof and other influencers can provide invaluable insights, motivation, and support. By engaging with these thought leaders, you can tap into a wealth of knowledge and experience, empowering you to overcome challenges and reach new heights in your personal growth.

WIM HOF, KNOWN AS THE "ICEMAN," has inspired millions with his revolutionary techniques, which combine breathwork, cold exposure, and mindset practices to unlock extraordinary physical and mental capabilities. By following his teachings and witnessing his accomplishments, you can gain a deeper understanding of the human body's potential and push yourself to break through perceived limitations. To stay connected with Wim Hof, subscribe to his social media channels, read his books, and participate in his workshops and events.

ASIDE FROM WIM HOF, there are countless other influencers and thought leaders who can inspire and guide you on your self-improvement journey. Tony Robbins, a renowned life and business strategist, is an excellent resource for those seeking motivation, empowerment, and practical strategies to overcome obstacles and achieve lasting success. Attend one of his events, read his books, or listen to his podcasts to benefit from his transformative insights and energy.

IF PHYSICAL HEALTH and fitness are your primary focus, consider following influencers like Kayla Itsines, a personal trainer and creator of the Bikini Body Guides. Her approachable fitness programs and encouraging presence on social media make her an ideal source of inspiration and guidance for those looking to improve their physical well-being.

FOR THOSE SEEKING A MORE holistic approach to wellness, look no further than Deepak Chopra, a pioneer in the field of integrative medicine and personal transformation. His teachings on meditation, mindfulness, and spiritual growth offer valuable insights and practical tools for cultivating inner peace and harmony. Engage with his content by reading his books, attending his events, or subscribing to his social media channels.

SOCIAL MEDIA PLATFORMS like Instagram and YouTube can be treasure troves of inspiration, offering a wealth of content from influencers across various fields. Be intentional in curating your feed, seeking out individuals who uplift, motivate, and educate you. In addition to established thought leaders, consider following lesser-known creators whose stories and experiences resonate with you on a personal level.

IT'S important to remember that no two self-improvement journeys are identical, and the influencers who inspire you may differ from those who resonate with others. Embrace your unique path by seeking out thought leaders who align with your values, goals, and passions. Be open to learning from diverse sources and adapting their teachings to suit your individual needs and circumstances.

As YOU ENGAGE with the content of these influencers and thought leaders, remember to maintain a balanced perspective, recognizing that they are human and fallible, just like everyone else. Take their insights and advice with a discerning eye, critically evaluating their teachings and applying them in a way that best serves your personal growth journey.

IN CONCLUSION, staying inspired by following Wim Hof and other influencers can provide a powerful catalyst for personal transformation, empowering you to overcome challenges, grow, and thrive. By engaging with these thought leaders and integrating their wisdom and experiences into your life, you can forge a unique path toward self-improvement, fueled by the inspiration and guidance of those who have gone before you.

Sharing Your Journey: Inspiring Others to Transform Their Lives

SHARING your journey can have a profound impact on the lives of others, inspiring them to embark on their own path of transformation and growth. As you openly share your experiences, challenges, and triumphs, you become a beacon of hope and encouragement for those who may be struggling or searching for direction in their lives.

ONE POWERFUL WAY TO share your story is by creating a blog or website that chronicles your experiences and insights. This digital platform allows you to connect with a global audience, offering a space for reflection, learning, and dialogue. As you write about your personal growth journey, consider incorporating lessons learned, strategies employed, and obstacles overcome to provide valuable guidance for your readers.

SOCIAL MEDIA PLATFORMS can also be excellent vehicles for sharing your journey and inspiring others. By regularly posting updates, photos, and reflections on platforms like Instagram, Facebook, or Twitter, you can create a visual and narrative record of your transformation. This real-time documentation not only motivates you to stay accountable but also encourages others to join you in pursuing a path of growth and self-improvement.

DON'T UNDERESTIMATE the power of personal connections in sharing your journey. Engage in meaningful conversations with friends, family, and acquaintances, discussing your experiences and the impact they've had on your life. These authentic interactions can be incredibly inspiring, fostering a sense of connection and understanding that transcends the digital realm.

PARTICIPATING in community events or joining local groups focused on personal growth can also provide opportunities for sharing your experiences and inspiring others. Whether it's a yoga class, a meditation group, or a workshop on personal development, these gatherings allow you to connect with like-minded individuals who may be motivated by your story.

PUBLIC SPEAKING IS another way to share your journey and inspire others. Consider offering to speak at conferences, schools, or community organizations about your experiences and the transformative power of personal growth. By stepping onto the stage and sharing your story, you can impact the lives of countless people, inspiring them to take action and pursue their own paths of self-improvement.

. . .

As you share your journey, remember that vulnerability is a strength, not a weakness. By being open and honest about your struggles, fears, and setbacks, you create a sense of relatability and authenticity that resonates with others. This honesty fosters trust and connection, encouraging others to embrace their own vulnerabilities and embark on their unique journeys of transformation.

Throughout this process, always remember to practice empathy and compassion, both for yourself and for those who may be inspired by your story. Recognize that everyone's path is different, and what works for you may not work for others. By approaching your own journey and the journeys of others with an open heart and a nonjudgmental mindset, you create a supportive environment in which transformation can truly flourish.

By sharing your journey and inspiring others to transform their lives, you not only contribute to their personal growth but also enrich your own experience. This reciprocal exchange of inspiration and encouragement creates a powerful ripple effect, touching the lives of countless individuals and fostering a collective movement toward positive change. Embrace the opportunity to share your story and be a source of hope, guidance, and motivation for those who may be searching for direction or inspiration in their own lives.

Living a Life of Purpose: The Impact of the Wim Hof Method on Overall Happiness and Fulfillment

Living a life of purpose is a quest that many pursue, and the Wim Hof Method has emerged as a powerful catalyst for achieving overall happiness and fulfillment. The method, pioneered by the "Iceman" Wim Hof, combines breathing techniques, cold exposure, and mindset exercises to foster physical, mental, and emotional resilience.

THE WIM HOF METHOD'S breathing exercises have a profound impact on our overall well-being. By consciously controlling our breath, we can regulate our stress response and tap into a state of calm and relaxation. This state not only boosts our immune system but also helps us manage anxiety and depression, leading to an increased sense of happiness and fulfillment.

COLD EXPOSURE, another pillar of the Wim Hof Method, challenges our bodies and minds in unique ways. By immersing ourselves in cold water or environments, we force our bodies to adapt and become more resilient. This adaptation process leads to increased energy levels, improved circulation, and a stronger immune system. As we conquer the cold, our self-confidence grows, and we develop a deeper sense of purpose and fulfillment.

THE THIRD COMPONENT of the Wim Hof Method focuses on cultivating a strong mindset. Through meditation and visualization, we can train our minds to become more resilient and adaptable, helping us face life's challenges with a positive attitude. This mental fortitude is key to living a life of purpose, as it allows us to navigate setbacks and obstacles with grace and perseverance.

INCORPORATING the Wim Hof Method into your daily routine can have a transformative effect on your life. As you become more in tune with your breath, body, and mind, you may notice a newfound sense of clarity and direction. This clarity can help you identify your passions and values, guiding you toward a life of purpose and fulfillment.

. . .

MANY INDIVIDUALS who have adopted the Wim Hof Method have reported profound improvements in their overall happiness and well-being. These testimonials serve as powerful reminders of the potential impact this method can have on our lives. By overcoming physical and mental challenges, we can unlock a deeper sense of self-awareness and purpose, leading to a more fulfilling and meaningful life.

FOR THOSE SEEKING to integrate the Wim Hof Method into their lives, it's essential to approach the practice with patience and persistence. Like any new skill or habit, it takes time and dedication to master the breathing techniques, cold exposure, and mindset exercises. Be kind to yourself as you embark on this journey, and celebrate each small victory along the way.

ONE OF THE most significant benefits of the Wim Hof Method is its accessibility. You don't need to invest in expensive equipment or travel to remote locations to experience its life-changing effects. By incorporating the breathing exercises, cold exposure, and mindset practices into your daily routine, you can begin to experience the transformative power of this method and unlock a life of purpose and happiness.

LIVING a life of purpose is a journey that requires consistent effort, self-reflection, and growth. The Wim Hof Method offers a unique and powerful toolset to help you cultivate resilience, self-awareness, and fulfillment. As you embrace this practice and experience its transformative effects, you'll be well on your way to creating a life that is both meaningful and joyful, inspiring others with your passion, dedication, and resilience.

CONCLUSION

The pursuit of happiness and fulfillment is a universal human endeavor, and the Wim Hof Method has emerged as a compelling means to foster this journey. Combining the power of breathwork, cold exposure, and mindset training, the method equips individuals with tools to enhance physical, mental, and emotional resilience. In doing so, it provides a path toward living a life of purpose and satisfaction, inspiring others along the way.

BREATHING, a seemingly simple act, holds immense potential to transform our lives. The Wim Hof Method's focus on breathwork allows us to access deeper states of relaxation and well-being. By consciously controlling our breath, we can regulate our stress response, bolster our immune system, and manage symptoms of anxiety and depression. This newfound sense of calm and balance empowers us to approach life's challenges with poise, opening the door to happiness and fulfillment.

COLD EXPOSURE, another integral aspect of the Wim Hof Method, pushes the boundaries of our comfort zones. By willingly subjecting ourselves to the cold, we trigger a cascade of physiological adaptations that improve our energy levels, circulation, and immune response. This process of overcoming physical discomfort strengthens our self-confidence and fosters a deeper sense of purpose and satisfaction.

THE THIRD CORNERSTONE of the Wim Hof Method, cultivating a strong mindset, is essential for navigating life's obstacles with resilience and optimism. By engaging in meditation and visualization exercises, we can train our minds to become more adaptable and tenacious. This mental fortitude is a crucial element in living a life of purpose, as it enables us to persevere in the face of setbacks and adversity.

AS INDIVIDUALS EMBRACE the Wim Hof Method and incorporate its principles into their daily routines, they often report a renewed sense of clarity and direction. This heightened self-awareness can help reveal passions and values, guiding people toward a life of purpose and fulfillment. By overcoming physical and mental challenges, individuals can unlock their true potential and lead lives rich in meaning and joy.

THE TRANSFORMATIVE IMPACT of the Wim Hof Method is evident in the countless testimonials of those who have adopted its practices. These inspiring stories serve as powerful reminders of the potential for growth and change inherent in each of us. By embracing the method and its principles, we can chart a course toward a life of purpose and happiness, inspiring others to follow in our footsteps.

FOR THOSE SEEKING to integrate the Wim Hof Method into their lives, patience and persistence are key. Like any new skill or habit, it takes time and dedication to master the breathing techniques, cold exposure, and mindset exercises. It is important to be gentle with oneself and to celebrate each small victory along the way.

. . .

ONE OF THE most appealing aspects of the Wim Hof Method is its accessibility. The practice does not require expensive equipment or exotic locations; its benefits can be experienced from the comfort of one's home. By incorporating the method's principles into daily life, anyone can begin to unlock its transformative potential and embark on a journey toward purpose and happiness.

THE WIM HOF METHOD offers a unique and powerful means to enhance resilience, self-awareness, and fulfillment. Its focus on breathwork, cold exposure, and mindset training provides a comprehensive toolkit for personal growth and development. As individuals adopt these practices and experience their transformative effects, they are better equipped to lead lives of purpose and joy.

LIVING a life of purpose is a continuous journey, one that requires consistent effort, self-reflection, and growth. The Wim Hof Method serves as a valuable ally in this quest, empowering individuals to cultivate the resilience, self-awareness, and satisfaction needed to create a meaningful and joyful existence. By embracing this practice and sharing its benefits with others, we can inspire those around us to pursue their own paths of transformation, collectively creating a world marked by happiness, fulfillment, and purpose.

Read the Rest of the Cold Exposure Mastery Series and Supercharge Your Body and Mind

BEYOND COLD SHOWERS
A Comprehensive Guide to the Wim Hof Method and Its Benefits

THE COLD WATER THERAPY BOOK
Guide to Cold Water Immersion, Ice Baths, and Showers for Improved Health, Recovery, Mental Resilience, Sleep Quality, and Enhanced Immune System

THE COLD PLUNGE CRYOTHERAPY BOOK
Diving Into the Healing Powers of Cold Water Exposure

Printed in Great Britain
by Amazon